FENG
风 POETRY CHINA

第一卷 风物诗

Copyright © 2017 Individual Authors and Translators
Compiling copyright © 2017 风 *FENG: Poetry China*
Photos © Individual Authors

风, pronounced "Feng" as in Fengshui, carries multiple meanings: wind, style, trend…

A magazine book (Mook)

Volume 1: WIND MATTERS
ISBN 9780982345931
Published by DJS BOOKS
FENG: Poetry China is a sister magazine with *Poetry East West*
www.poetryeastwest.com

编辑：　《风》诗刊编委会
出版：　DJS 书社
日期：　2017 年 5 月 4 日第一次印刷
网站：　www.poetryeastwest.com

《风》，以书代刊，向外译介当代中国诗，2016 年 12 月创刊
《诗东西》，以诗人互译的形式双向译介，2010 年 10 月创刊

Contents

I. Wind from Eight Directions

001/ Poems by Song Wei   (Sichuan)
033/ Poems by Zhu Zhu   (Nanjing)
065/ Poems by Han Bo   (Shanghai)
085/ Poems by Ming Di   (California)
115/ Poems by Song Lin   (Yunnan)
141/ Poems by Yang Xiaobin   (Taiwan)
169/ Poems by Zang Di   (Beijing)
201/ Poems by Meng Ming   (Paris)

II. Essays, Reviews and Interviews

221/ Zang Di: Is there a crisis in Chinese New Poetry?
231/ Xiaobin: A poetic essay interrupted by Yang
233/ Zhu Zhu: Take it along
235/ Song Wei: The book has been read—remembering a dream
237/ Su Xuan: A moment of life at sunset
245/ Ming Di: Re-reading Hu Shi
263/ Interviews: Jing Wendong, Sen Zi, Sang Ke, Jiang Tao,
                Jiang Hao, Zheng Xiaoqiong, Zhu Yu, Qin Sanshu
275/ Reviews: Li Sen, Xi Du, Chen Jun, Ni Zhijuan, etc.
291/ Editorial: Which wind the witch dances in, east west, east?

目录

1. 八面来风

001/ 宋炜诗选（中/英）

033/ 朱朱诗选（中/英）

065/ 韩博诗选（中/英）

085/ 明迪诗选（中/英/荷）

115/ 宋琳诗选（中/英）

141/ 杨小滨诗选（中/英）

169/ 臧棣诗选（中/英/印/西）

201/ 孟明诗选（中/法）

2. 随笔 评论 访谈

221/ 臧棣：关于新诗危机的一次对话（中/英）

231/ 杨小滨：一篇被法镭搅了局的诗论

233/ 朱朱：带着它往这边来

235/ 宋炜：书已读完——记一个梦

237/ 蔌弦：人世经停夕光片刻——略读韩博

245/ 明迪：重读胡适

263/ 访谈：敬文东 森子 桑克 姜涛
　　　　　蒋浩 郑小琼 茱萸 秦三澍等

275/ 译读：李森 西渡 陈均 倪志娟等

291/ 编后：风乎舞雩，东西东兮

Poems by Song Wei 宋炜诗选

Translations by Ming Di and Kerry Shawn Keys

宋炜，四川省沐川县人。1980年代期间与兄长宋渠共同署名发表了一些诗作，并参与发起"整体主义"诗歌活动。1990年代以后，独立署名发表作品。现居重庆。2016年获得DJS-诗东西颁发的首届"胡适诗歌奖"。

SONG Wei (1964-) is a poet from Muchuan County, Sichuan Province. He started publishing poems in the 1980s and was part of the Holistic poetry group from 1984 to 1989 in Chengdu. Since 1990 he has published poems under his own name. For many years he has escaped notice like a hermit until poets and critics re-discovered him recently. He was awarded the first "Hu Shi Poetry Prize" by DJS-*Poetry East West* in 2016. Currently he lives in Chongqing.

登高

其一

我在峰顶观天下，自视甚高；
普天之下，我不作第二人想；
日出只在我眼中，别无他人看到；
日落也是我一人的；
我走出身体，向下飞，
什么也触不到。
我才是世上第一个不死的人。

    2008.05.05

其二

在山上，我猎取的不是树木
或林间兽。
我只砍伐黄金、白银与青铜。
我在巅顶目击的
也不是太阳从云间的喷涌，
而是太阳系
在头顶的徐徐升起。

    2009.11.07

Climbing High

1.

I look at the world from a mountain top,
feeling high. Under the heaven there's no one else
but me. The sun rises in my eyes. No one else can see it.
The sun sets for me and only me.
I walk out of this body and fly down
but there is nothing down there for me to touch.
I'm the first human in this world, undying.

2.

I go hunting in the mountains
but not for wood or beasts.
I hunt for gold, silver, and bronze.
What I witness from the mountain top
is not the sun spewing from clouds
but the entire solar system
slowly rising above my head.

晚景小记

我回到乡下,看见自己与许多红辣椒一道
在场坝上晒太阳。我们把夏天搞得有多热啊。
我手搭凉篷,就以为在眼前安装了空调?
事实上,我的额角与颈子出产了许多盐。
看,我们还把这个夏天搞得如此咸湿!
并且,我对自己的款待也不尽人情,不然
我为什么要让自己斟上这一只满杯?
是的,因为我好不容易才有了半杯。
作为一个古旧的整体主义者,我要求
一切都是完备的,包括残云、余烬与垂死。
其实我也可以退而求其次:没有晚年。
这世上有太多人为了成为先驱而放弃了下半生。
一生太短,无法容纳,还不如抽身离去。
我如此极端,要不然飞起来吃人,要不然
就潜到海底看星星——天塌了,海水也溢满陆地。
如果我自己的衰老与地球暗合,为什么
我们的末日不能是同一天?假若地球等不及我这个
急切而甜蜜的大限,我会对世界说:请提前!

  2007

Small Notes in My Old Age

I return to the village and see lots of red peppers
sunbathing on the threshing floor with me,
giving warmth to the summer.
I put my hands to my eyebrow to make an arbor
as if installing an air conditioner in front of my eyes.
In fact, my forehead and my neck are making salt.
Lots of salt. Look, we've made this summer so salty!
And I'm not hospitable enough to myself, otherwise
why should I bring myself this full cup of liquor?
Yes, because I've finally had half of it.
As an antique holistic idealist, I demand everything be complete
including remnants of clouds, embers and death.
However, I can accept what's second best: no old age.
Too many people give up the rest of their lives to be a martyr.
One life is too short to accommodate, might as well leave.
I am so extreme. I either fly up to eat people, or dive
into the sea to watch the stars – the sky collapses,
sea water overflowing. If my old age coincides with this earth,
why aren't we doomed on the same day? If the earth can't wait
for my urgent but sweet deadline, I will say to the world:
Come sooner!

2007

沐川县纪事：
下南道的农事书或人物志

0

站在灰云下更灰的屋顶，
手扶避雷针，他鸟瞰多雨的沐川县：
糖果厂多么甜，豆瓣厂多么咸，
米仓多么香，仓鼠多么肥，
木桩间的阴影多么寂静，
电线上的鸟多么黑，
自行车多么远。

1

樱桃树下，那一片园中的小菜畦
还保持着零乱的翠绿吗？
斑鸠，山兔，岩鹰，猫头鹰，
蛞蝓，柴虫，塘中的鱼，还有飞碟
不时在对面的山岭上降落，
带来与梦境混同的可疑的光。
而在纱窗上练习攀岩的壁虎
有一天跌落于酒坛中。

Muchuan County Chronicle:
The Book of People or Rural Affairs in the Southern Basin

0

Standing under the gray clouds, on a grayer roof,
he holds a lightning rod and takes a bird's-eye view
of his rainy Muchuan County:
candy factories are sweet, bean factories are salty,
rice warehouses smell fragrant, and mice are fat.
Shadows between the wooden stakes are quiet.
Birds on the electric power lines are black.
Bicycles travel a long way.

1

Under a cherry tree, there was a small vegetable patch.
Is it still green but unkempt?
There are turtledoves, mountain rabbits, mountain eagles,
owls, slugs, and wood beetles. And fish in the pond.
And flying saucers
that fly across from the mountains from time to time
bringing suspicious light mixed with fragments of dreams.
And the gecko that used to practice climbing hills
on my window screens
finally falls one day into my liquor jar.

2

更多小人滑倒在田埂上。春雨如油
让他一病难起,甦醒时
随手撬折耳根疗疾。
赤脚医生踩踏软泥前来,足心一痛
一块骨朵般的茨菇被唤醒。
桑树上,空空的双肺迎风悬挂,
春天的翠绿沿着叶脉或肺脉
钻进心底,再和芽一起冒出头顶。
铜人就这样长出乱发,*丝丝如注*
头皮风凉而白净,双目也通明。
阡陌间,村庄细小而清晰,一生都被看完。
他看春天具体而微,就是一桶井水,
一篾桑叶,一树樱桃,一场凉*丝丝*的雨。

2

And more villains fall over the terraced ridge.
Spring rain falls like cooking oil.
He falls ill. When he finally wakes up,
he digs fishy smelling herbs to treat his ear.
A barefoot doctor walks over the loamy soil.
When he hurts his sole,
a bone-shaped mushroom wakes up.
On the mulberry tree, empty lungs hang in the wind.
The jade-green of Spring glissades through the lungs
into the heart and shoots out with buds and sprouts.
The Bronze Man* grows messy hair this way,
his scalp cool and clean, his eyes bright.
The village is small with terraced rice paddies,
everything so clear you can see right through your life.
He looks at Spring in detail, a bucket of well-water,
a basket of mulberry leaves, a tree full of cherries,
cool rain with clear threads of rain water.

*The ancient Chinese poet Li He (790–816) had a well-known poem about the Bronze Man made by Han Emperor Wudi (156-87 BCE) to catch the dew from the moon as an elixir of immortality. (Translator's note)

3

学习巫术，观师时
他看见农村的表叔一边喝酒
一边念观音咒。后者的小儿子
摔坏了腿，于是他含了一口井水
像喷叶子烟一样，将水雾
洒向小儿子的坏腿：腿立时
变成了翅膀或轮子，满院里乱飞。
这小哪吒一晃就没有了踪影。
他余兴未了，又朝天井
吐一泡口水，于是邻居的中饭
煮到晚上还是一锅生米。
他啊，高高兴兴喝他自己的小酒。

3

He tries to learn witchcraft and observes
what the village masters do.
His uncle chants curses while drinking.
He spits well-water at his youngest son,
the one with the broken legs.
The water sprays like tobacco smoke.
The broken legs immediately become wings or wheels
flying around the courtyard.
And the little rebel soon dashes away without a trace.
Still his uncle is not satisfied.
He spits saliva in the yard. His neighbors are cooking lunch
but by dinner time their lunch is still not ready –
raw rice in the wok, which makes him happy.
He drinks his liquor, contented.

4

他在河边饮水,喝入了几条小鱼。
他像一只盛装清水的杯盏
在盈满;不,他像一只透明的人形鱼缸
在换水。一尾小鱼在穿越他肺叶的
血腥水草,一粒蝌蚪
在等待流水莫须有的四只腿。
他也如蝌蚪一样,以为所有的水生物
都会长成女人;他还想如灯草和尚一般
轮番住进她们的身体,
在那些温暖的水草间穿行。
他呀,识得她们的水性,在里头游刃有余。
而她们继续潜行,鱼翔浅底,
浑不觉这隐秘的乐趣
正令她们加速,直上了青云里。

4

He drinks water by the river and swallows
a few small fish. Like a cup he is filling himself
with clear water. No, like a human-shaped fish tank
he is changing water, transparent.
A small fish swims through the bloody water plants
inside his lungs. A tadpole is waiting
to grow four groundless legs. Like a tadpole,
he expects all aquatic creatures to grow into women.
He would like to take turns living in their bodies,
one at a time, like the Grass Monk.* He would swim serenely
between the warm bodies remembering each of them.
And they would continue to submerge, their fins sweeping
the shallow bottom without knowing that the secret fun
is speeding them up – to the blue clouds.

*Grass Monk is an erotic character from the Qing dynasty novel
Strange Stories by Pu Songling (1640-1715). (Translator's note)

5

他在草台上搭起一个班子
搬演一部川剧。他不变脸,却一心听
幕后帮腔的高音,比绣花针更像一个奸细。
他的体态如空气,只有通过
光线的变化或光景的迁移
才能偶尔得以一瞥:全然是白花花的飘影。
但他实在是如此轻盈,几乎不在原地。
只有更美的娇娘能挽住他的闪烁,以及
他的定睛。这时节哪一个才是看客?
好呀,他的轻薄与跳脱如一个孙悟空的筋斗云,想当初
浪子燕青也不过如此。

5

He sets up a theater group on the grass stage
to put on a Sichuan Opera. His face motionless.*
A high-pitch voice comes from behind the scene,
thin and sharp, trickier than an embroidery needle.
His body moves so light, like air, you can catch a glimpse
of him only when the light changes: a floating shadow.
Indeed he is so light, almost not touching the floor.
Only the beautiful females can hold his flickering
and his gaze. In this season who is the spectator?
Well, his slim body performs somersaults like the Monkey King.
Even the prodigal Yanqing in the Water Margin fiction
was no better than this.

* Sichuan opera is one of the oldest forms of performing art in China that revived in the 20th century. The main feature is "face changing" where the actors change their masks quickly like a magic. (Translator's note)

6

他经过白铁铺子,金属闪光,铁砧乱响。
他自己就像个白铁铺子,收集了街面上所有的光,
比太阳还明亮。
他趿着木屐,吊儿郎当地,他一个人的游荡
比整个集市还要拥挤。
为了让钱财进一步迷糊他的心窍,
他不见棺材不掉泪:棺材
只是另一具盛装粮食的方斗,
而泪水是浇淋棺木的养分。
他越山涉水,扛上这只斗去走山。
为了收租或收尸,他像个
撵阴的地理先生
走遍了房山和旗山。

6

He passes by blacksmith shops, white metals flash.
He himself is a metal shop collecting all the light,
brighter than the sun.
He slops on wooden clogs, slovenly. Wandering alone,
he crowds the entire market.
He wants to indulge in money and harden his heart,
not shedding tears in front of coffins.
Coffins are just containers for rice, in different shapes.
Tears can shine and polish the coffins.
He crosses mountains and waters with a rice container.
He collects the rent or corpses.
He has traveled all over Mt. Fang and Mt. Qi
like a Mr. Geography chasing ghosts.

7

他曾经有一怀清洁的肺，寂静的呼吸
吹动过水面上风车斗转的轮子；
如今他的双肺中长满杂草，
含金量如一只割草的镰刀在锈蚀。
他心中的福田如今只是山腰里
一个单身女观音的庙产：泥胎中的
泥心与泥肺，离真身有多远？
连丰收也未能激起他古老的性欲。
呀，收割后的田间充满了蟋蟀干旱的叫喊。

7

He used to have clean lungs and his quiet breathing
could turn windmills over the water's surface.
Now weeds have grown and filled his lungs.
His body rusts like a rusty sickle that cuts weeds.
His field of happiness lies beyond, on the hillside
temple of a female Buddha who is still single.
Clay heart and clay lungs in a clay body.
How far is it from the real body?
Even the harvest fails to arouse his ancient desire.
Yeah, the field after harvest teems with the parched cry
of crickets.

8

这些都是游戏中的深奥知识:
侧耳倾听响簧的音律,注目于
陀螺晕眩的旋转,以双脚
践约跳房子时的风水流程;
或以木头人自比,失却了提绳的牵引。
时光就藏在这些事物中间。
如今他用一只探照灯
向其照射,时光又现身于这些
一一掠过的聚光下,并暴露出
它们未曾磨损的质地。
而提线的手埋伏在墙角的暗影中
等待他的重临。
转个弯,只须一个回首,
昨天保持原样,在台阶上等他回家。
家人们正把猪油揉进雪白的泡粑。

8

This is the profound knowledge of the game:
Listen to the sound of the reed, pay attention
to the yo-yo's spellbound spinning, jump with two feet
to get the tricky Feng Shui when practicing hopscotch,
or claim to be a wooden puppet without a string attached.
Time is concealed in the middle of all of these.
Now he's holding a searchlight to find them.
Time resurfaces from there –
it exposes their texture under the spotlight,
not worn out yet,
while the hand that holds the string in the shadow
awaits his return.
Turn around and look back,
yesterday remains there, waiting for him on his porch.
His folks are kneading lard into white sponge cakes.

9

此刻,他头戴宝塔形高帽,脚踩高跷
像云朵一样掠过头顶,一晃
就到了凉桥;我得以仰望他开衩的裤裆,
听睾丸一阵乱响;
此刻,他乘纸鸢到来,
我追着他地上一路滑行的影子,
他飞越城墙的一刻,我架上云梯
坐在旗杆顶端的旗斗里,去摸他鹞尾似的衣袂。
我猜他怀中揣着一张鲁班先师的绣像。
就这样,他并不借力助跑
起身踏上云端,看见了
落日在远山间的盛宴。
也有别的人目睹了这盛大的一刻。君不见:
一只小阳雀,
飞过沐溪河;
站在花枝上,
看倒太阳落。①

① 所引为贵州山歌。第二句原文为"乌江河",此处置换为"沐溪河"。

9

Right now he's wearing a pagoda-shaped cap,
his feet on peg stilts. He crosses overhead
like a cloud and reaches the cool bridge.
I look up to see the split crotch of his pants,
and I can hear his balls bursting chaos.
At this moment he has returned to me on a paper kite.
I chase his sliding shadow.
When he flies over the wall, I climb up the cloud ladder
and sit down on top of the flagpole. I touch
the long bird-tail of his shirt. I guess
he is holding an embroidered portrait of master Luban.*
And so he walks into the clouds, just like that,
and sees the sunset feasting in the distant mountains.
Other people have also witnessed this grand moment:
"A sunny bird quivers
flying over the Mu Rivers.
On a twig of flowers
it catches the sunset hours."

① The cited four lines are from a Guizhou folk song, except that the original "Wu Rivers" is replaced by "Mu Rivers". (Author's note)

* Luban (c. 507–444 BCE) was an ancient Chinese carpenter and inventor, revered as the Chinese God of carpentry. He invented the cloud ladder and wooden bird. (Translator's note)

0

多年以后的这个三月
他已不再伤春或病酒。
一切都变了,他不再能
倾听植物抽芽或开花的语言,
因为他的头脑中全是用生铁
铸就的一块砧,但缺少哪怕是
零星的敲击。如今他的春天
在体外,在来世不及的
另一次生活中,或者
在从前的某个三月。
有时,他用一种寂静的声音唱歌,
歌声虽小,但很清晰,
仿佛远到天边的人也能听见;
有时,他专注于内心不为人知的
欢乐,用黄雀、蟋蟀或阵雨的语言
保持沉默。在那个春天,
他对面的旗山是神仙的世界,
他的身体是一座花园。

  2003.04.04-12,初记
  2015.10.14,重抄

0

Now it's March again, many years afterwards.
He is no longer sentimental about Spring,
or getting sick on liquor. Things have changed.
He can no longer hear the flowering language of plants.
His mind is a wedge of pig iron,
nothing knocks to wake it up. His Spring is outside
of his body, in another life
that not even his afterlife can reach.
One March sometime in the past,
he sang in a silent voice, faint but clear, as if
even people from as far away as the horizon could hear.
Sometimes he focused on things unnoticed by others,
small joys, voices of orioles, crickets and showers of rain.
He kept silent for them. It was that Spring
that he faced Mt. Qi, the fairytale land.
His body was a garden.

2003, 2015

金缕曲：一只老而小的悲歌

到现在为止，你对我来说是一个身体，
但我要你拥有更多身体，一个大身体。
你吸引了山脉与流云，像那只
怀孕的、田纳西州的坛子，高高鼓起。
我可以住进去。我也可以顺带着
把一片草原放进你的身体，把蜜桃林
种进你胸前双乳正在拉开的抽屉里。
唯一可以航行的地方是你的血液（它是 B 型的）。
我不想到别处去寻找另一个好子宫。
但我用什么迎接你：灰心、性病和赤贫？
我是谁？一个外来者，却拥有
和你丈夫和儿子都有的要求，也许，还有父亲的。
既然万物无常，拥有即失去
我也可以安于现状：永不得到你。
你看我，鞭长莫及，又洋洋得意。
我在园子里晾衣时，也会把
这首诗用夹子晾在风里。
我对自己的问候是：早安，老爷！
早安，阿斯匹宁！早安，安定！
但是，你不止是有身体，你还有
比身体更虚无的前世和小历史。

Tune of the Golden Thread: an old, small elegy

So far you are one body to me
but I want you to be more bodies. A big body
that attracts mountains and floating clouds,
like a pregnant jar, the jar in Tennessee, high up.
I'm moving in to live there. I'm bringing a meadow
into your body, a peach orchard
into the chest your breasts are opening.
The only place one can sail is in your blood (type B).
I don't want to go anywhere else to find
another delectable uterus. But how do I greet you?
With frustration, sexual disease, and extreme poverty?
Who am I? An outsider, but possessing the desires
your husband and son would have, and your father too.
But nothing is permanent. To possess is to lose.
I might as well be content of never having you.
Look, I'm beyond reaching you, but feel triumphant.
When I dry my clothes in the yard, I take this poem
and hang it in the wind with a clothespin.
I greet myself: Good morning Master!
Good morning Aspirin! Good morning peacefulness!
But you are more than a body. You are your previous life
and a small history that's more meaningless than a body.

作为一个探险者，不，一个考古学家
我要你的体内的废墟、骨殖和血脉。
对于这些，我要么落空，要么兼得。
我并不满足于做一个见缝插针的奸细
或见猎与见色时都要心喜若狂的刺客。
我要进去，我要探索你繁复的下水，
一套良好的设备总成，一个好子宫。
虽然你远远的在京师，像一个宫殿，
但进去后我才发现里面空无一物，我
想象中的未来并不在那儿等待。
你身体的深处是一个空舞台，甚至你自己
也没在那儿起舞。我要的正是这空无。
我的幻想与虚构正在入侵你的身体。
这不是一般的意淫，不被对方感知。
而你能。你正经受着我的进入，
用你的空，来抚慰我更加空无的幻觉。
这种力量，有如业力，当然，天生有
欲力的向度，使 Karma 和 Kama 在一瞥之间①
被你混淆一体。这也使你的空
变得空前具体，就像你的小球耳环，
悬浮或漂摇着，如一只中空的行星。
而你的手镯打造得辛苦，是一个空心的银河系。
我每次看你，犹如仰望一个正在运行的天体：
当月亮净身，它从不用水，而是
隔着整片天空去引用地球上的潮汐。

As an explorer, no, as an archaeologist
I want the ruins, the bones and bloodline in your body.
I'll either fail, or get them all.
I'm not satisfied just to be a spy taking a rare chance
or an assassin that gets wildly happy with his prey.
I want to go in. I want to explore your complicated insides,
the well-equipped innards, the exquisite uterus.
You are like a palace far away in the capital.
When I go in I find nothing. The imagined future
is not waiting there. There is an empty stage
deep in your body but even your own very self
is not dancing there. All I want is exactly this emptiness.
I'm invading your body with my fiction and fantasies.
This is not an ordinary obscenity. It's not to be sensed
by anyone but you. You are experiencing my invasion.
With your emptiness you soothe my emptier illusion.
This power is Karma, but, of course, also naturally Kama,
both blended into one body, Karma Kama. ①
It makes your emptiness so concrete and singular,
like your ball-shaped earing
suspended in the air or drifting, a hollow planet.
And your bracelet, made so sturdy, a hollow galaxy.
Every time I see you, I see you as if looking up at a moving
  object:
the moon doesn't purify itself with water
but with the ocean tides across the entire sky.

于是，你的身体不再只是你自己，
还有山脉、流云，和更多美丽的邻居：你身上
没有什么是不可以融入万物的。
由此，你的身体值得占有无穷的丝绸与布帛，
但我不要这些，我只要那一个：
你的值得我独自占有的大身体。
你来了，用一条大街来传导你的气息
（如果我站得更远，你会用掉一个银河系）；
你走了，世界顿时空空如也；
你朝我转身，仿佛离去的万物又都随你归来。
唯有你，能使菜市场和小酒馆熠熠生辉，
也唯有菜市场和小酒馆，才能拯救我的灵魂。
即使这并非遗言，我也要对你说：
我之等候你，好比一个酒鬼之苦等酒熟——
是的，死疲塌赖地，我就是要喝到这一口，
我宁愿守在天锅旁，死在出酒三分钟以后。

①梵语的英译：karma，业力。Kama，欲力。

    2008.05.27，初记于袁家岗
    2015.10.17，重抄于沙坪坝

So your body is no longer just your own, you have to count
mountains, clouds, and many more beautiful neighbors:
there is nothing that cannot be integrated into everything.
Therefore your body is worth possessing,
worthy of endless silk and cloth.
But I don't want any of these. I want just one:
your ample body that deserves my possession.
Here you come, with a whole street transmitting your breath
(if I stand farther away, you'll occupy the whole galaxy).
There you go, the entire world is suddenly emptied.
You turn toward me, everything gone with you is returning.
Only you can stir up markets and restaurants
and only markets and small restaurants can save my soul.
Even though this is not my final will and testament, I have to
    say:
I have been waiting for you like a drunkard
waiting for the drink to ferment—
Yes, shamelessly, I just want to taste this drink.
I'll wait for the nectar in the jar,
          and die three minutes after it's brewed.

2008, 2015

① Sanskrit in English translation: karma, poetic justice; Kama, desire. (Author's note)

风 Feng 32

POEMS BY ZHU ZHU 朱朱诗选

李栋英译 Translations by Dong Li

朱朱，诗人，艺术评论家，策展人，出生于江苏扬州，出版有著作多种，其中包括诗集《枯草上的盐》、《皮箱》、《故事》、《青烟》（法文版，译者 Chantal Chen-Andro），艺术评论《灰色的狂欢节——2000年以来的中国当代艺术》等，曾获安高诗歌奖，中国当代艺术奖评论奖（CCAA）。先后受邀于法国 Val-de-Marne 国际诗歌节，美国 Henry Luce 基金会中国诗歌翻译项目，英文版诗集《野长城》（译者李栋）将于2017年由美国 Phoneme Media 出版社出版。

ZHU Zhu was born in Yangzhou, P.R. China. He is a poet, critic and curator of art exhibitions and has published numerous volumes of poetry and prose, such as *Drive to Another Planet*, *Salt on Wilted Grass*, *Blue Smoke*（French, tr. by Chantal Chen-Andro）, *The Trunk*, *Stories*, *Vertigo*, and *Grey Carnival—Chinese Contemporary Art since 2000*. Zhu's honors include Anne Kao poetry prizes, the French International Poetry Val-de-Marne Fellowship, Chinese Contemporary Art Award for Critics and Henry Luce Foundation Chinese Poetry Fellowship at the Vermont Studio Center. The *Wild Great Wall* will be published by Phoneme Media in late 2017.

野长城

I

地球表面的标签
或记忆深处的一道勒痕,消褪在
受风沙和干旱的侵蚀
而与我们的肤色更加相似的群山。

我们曾经在这边。即使
是一位征召自小村镇的年轻士兵,
也会以直立的姿势与富有者的心情
透过箭垛打量着外族人,
那群不过是爬行在荒原上的野兽。

在这边,我们已经营造出一只巨大的浴缸,
我们的日常是一种温暖而慵倦的浸泡。
当女人们在花园里荡秋千,
男人们的目光嗜好于从水中找到倒影;

带血的、未煮熟的肉太粗俗了,
我们文明的屋檐
已经精确到最后那一小截的弯翘。

the wild great wall

I

label of the earth surface
or a strangled trace deep in memory, vanishing
upon invasion of sand-storms and droughts
into mountains whose skin tone is ever closer to ours.

we were once here. even
a young solider conscripted from a small town
would stand tall and with the heart of a rich man
judge aliens through piles of arrows,
the herd of people, no better than beasts crawling in wasteland.

here, we have already built a giant bathtub,
to soak ourselves in warm and languid routine.
when women play on a swing in the garden,
men's eyes seek out reflections in the water;

barely-cooked bloody meat too uncouth,
the eaves of our civilization
now exacting to the last stretch of an upward tip.

II

现在,经历着
所有的摧毁中最彻底的一种:
遗忘——它就像

一头爬行动物的脊椎
正进入风化的尾声,
山脊充满了侏罗纪的沉寂,
随着落日的遥远马达渐渐地平息,
余晖像锈蚀的箭镞坠落。

我来追溯一种在我们出生前就消失的生活,
如同考据学的手指苦恼地敲击
一只空壳的边沿,
它的内部已经掏干了。

II

now, go through
the most thorough of all destructions:
forgetting—it is like

a reptile spine
moving toward the end of its weathering,
mountain ridges full of jurassic quietude,
as the setting sun moves away, the engine dies slowly down,
the remnant light falls like rusty arrows.

i come to trace the life that disappeared long before our birth,
as if the philological fingers knock in anguish
the ridge of an empty shell,
whose inside has been picked clean.

III

在陡坡的那几棵桃树上，
蜜蜂们哼着歌来回忙碌着，
它们选择附近的几座
就像摔破的陶罐般的烽火台
做为宿营地。

那歌词的大意仿佛是：
一切都还给自然……

野草如同大地深处的手指，
如同蓬勃的、高举矛戟的幽灵部队
登上了坍塌的台阶，
这样的时辰，无数受惊的风景
一定正从各地博物馆的墙壁上仓惶地逃散。

III

in the peach trees on the steep slope,
bees hum and buzz around,
they have set up a campsite
in a nearby beacon tower
that has been smashed like crockery.

their song seems to say:
everything returns to nature...

wild grass like fingers deep in the earth,
like a fiery ghost troop with halberds and lances held high
climbs onto collapsed steps,
this moment, countless startled landscapes
must be fluttering and fleeing off the walls from museums
everywhere.

first appeared in The Brooklyn Rail

青烟

I

清澈的刘海；
发髻盘卷，
一个标准的小妇人。
她那张椭圆的脸，像一只提前
报答了气候的水蜜桃。

跷起腿，半转身躯，一只手肘撑在小桌子上，
手指夹住一支燃烧的香烟（烟燃尽，
有人会替她续上一支，再走开）。在屋中
她必须保持她的姿势至终，
摄影师走来走去，画家盯住自己的画布，
一只苍蝇想穿透玻璃飞出，最后看得她想吐。

晚上她用一条包满冰的毛巾敷住手臂。

blue smoke

I

clear bangs;
a coiled bun,
a standard little lady.
her oval face looks like a peach
that repays the climate ahead of its time.

crossing her legs, turning her body half-way around, an elbow
    on a small table,
a burning cigarette between her fingers (once the cigarette is finished,
someone will hand her another one and then walk away). in the room
she must maintain her posture until the end,
a photographer walks back and forth, a painter stares at his canvas,
a fly wants to fly through the glass, she watches and wants to vomit.

at night, she wraps her arms with a towel of ice.

II

第二天接着干。又坐在
小圆凳上,点起烟。画家
和她低声交谈了几句,问她的祖籍、姓名。
摄影师没有来,也许不来了?
透过画家背后的窗,可以望见外滩。
江水打着木桩。一艘单桅船驶向对岸荒岛上。

一辆电车在黄包车铃声里掣过。她
想起冠生园软软的座垫,想着自己
不够浑圆的屁股,在上边翘得和黑女人一样高。
这时她忘记了自己被画着,往常般吸一口烟,

烟圈徐徐被吐出。
被挡在画架后面的什么哐啷地一声。
画家黑黝黝的眼窝再次对准了她,吓了
她一跳。她低下头扯平
已经往上翻卷到大腿根的旗袍。
这一天过得快多了。

II

they continue to work the next day. she sits again
on the small round stool, lights a cigarette. the painter
talks to her briefly in a low voice, and asks where she comes
    from and her name.
the photographer has not come yet, perhaps he will not come?
through the window behind the painter's back, she can see
    the bund. the river
beats upon wood stakes. a sloop sails toward the deserted island
    on the other shore.

a trolley rushes by in the ringing of the rickshaw bell. she
thinks of soft cushions at guanshengyuan, thinks of her bottom
that is not round enough, not as bubbly as a black lady's.
now she forgets that she is being painted, and continues to
    smoke,

rings of smoke slowly spit out.
something behind the easel bangs on the ground.
the painter's shady eyeholes scrutinize her again and startle
her. she lowers her head, while smoothing
over the cheongsam that has already curled up the deep of her
    thighs.
today it goes by much faster.

III

此后几天她感觉自己
不必盛满她的那个姿势,或者
完全就让它空着。

她坐在那里,好像套着一层
表情的模壳,薄薄的,和那件青花旗袍一样。
在模壳的里边——
她已经在逛街,已经
懒洋洋地躺在了一张长榻上分开了双腿
大声的打呵欠,已经
奔跑在天边映黄了溪流的油菜田里。

摄影师又出现过一次。
把粗壮奇长的镜头伸出
皮革机身,近得几乎压在她脸上,
她顺势给他一个微笑,甜甜的。

一台电唱机:
"蔷薇蔷薇处处开";①
永春和②派人送来 陪伴他们的工作。

---

① 20 世纪三十年代盛行上海滩的百乐门爵士歌曲之一。
② 全称为永春和烟草股份有限公司,即雇用诗中的妓女做广告模特儿的商家。

III

the next few days she feels
that she does not have to be fully present in her posture, or
leave it completely inattentive.

she sits there, as if wrapped
in a thin mask of expression, thin as her blue and white
    colored cheongsam.
inside the mask—
she is already wandering the streets, already
lies lazily on a long couch and parts her legs
yawning in a loud voice, already
runs in the canola fields by the edge of the sky that yellows
    the streams.

the photographer appears once again.
the thick and unbelievably long lens pokes out
of the leathered body, so close that it presses on her face,
she yields and smiles him a sweet smile.

a record player:
"rose rose blossoms everywhere":1
yongchunhe2 sends someone over to keep them company.

---

[1] a paramont jazz song popular on the bund in shanghai during the 1930s
[2] full name is yongchunhe tobacco corporation, namely the firm that hired the prostitute in the poem as their advertising model.

IV

她开始跑出那个模壳,
站到画家的身边打量那幅画:
画中人既像又不像她,
他在她的面颊上涂抹了太多的胭脂,
夹烟的手画得过于纤细,
他画的乳房是躲在绸衣背后而不是从那里鼓胀,
并且,他把她背影里的墙
画成一座古怪的大瀑布
僵立着但不流动。
唯独从她手指间冒起的一缕烟
真的很像在那里飘,在空气中飘。

她还发现这个画家
其实很早就画完了这幅画,
在后来很长的一段日子里,每天
他只是在不停地涂抹那缕烟。

IV

she starts to run out of the mask,
and stands by the painter to see the painting:
the lady in the painting looks like and not like her,
he puts on too much make-up on her face,
the hand that holds the cigarette too delicate,
her breasts in his painting hide instead of bulging under her
    silk clothes
and he paints the wall in her shadow
as a strange waterfall
stiff and static.
only a wisp of smoke that rises from between her fingers
which looks as if it floats, floating in the air.

she also finds out that this painter
in fact has long finished the painting,
and the long days after, every day
he does nothing but fiddle with that wisp of smoke.

first appeared in The Brooklyn Rail

爬墙虎

她是疯狂的，柔软的手掌
已经蜕变成虎爪和吸盘，
从最初的一跃开始，覆盖，
层层叠叠，吞没整面墙，缝合
整个屋子，黯淡下全部光线；
从不退缩，即使步入了虚空
也会变成一队螺旋形的盾牌；
即使入冬后枝叶全部枯萎，仍然
用缝纫线被抽走后留下的成串针孔
镶嵌自己的身形；她有僵持的决心，
被粉碎的快感，和春天到来时
那一份膨胀的自我犒劳，如同
在沙盘里插上密密的小旗，
如同蜂拥的浪尖以为扎破了礁岩；
她是绝望的，无法进入到屋中，
但她至少遮蔽了外面的一切，
年复一年，她是真的在爱着。

the creeper

she runs wild, soft palms
now morphed to tiger claws and suckers
which, from the first leap, cover,
overlay, devour the whole wall, stitch up
the whole room, dim all the lights;
she never backs off; even if stepping into a void
will turn into a shield of corkscrews;
even if all the leaves wilt in winter, she still
decorates her body with a string of holes
after the sewing threads are pulled out;
her tenacity holds up in a stalemate, she takes pleasure
in being crushed, and her self-congratulation expands in spring
like tightly-spaced pennants stuck in a sandbox
as if thorny waves think they have slit the shoal;
she despairs, unable to enter the room
but at least she camouflages everything outside:
year after year, she truly loves.

first appeared in Asia Literary Review

石窟

落日无法追赶，
我们到达时天已经暗去。
地轴吱嘎的转动声响彻在两岸之间，
整条河好像被埋进幽深的洞穴，
只能隔着悬浮的地平线倾听。

旅馆在山顶——
一条曾经萦回在白居易暮年的山道，
积满了无法再回到枝头的落叶；
在旅馆的登记簿上，
我们的一生被判决为外乡人。

眺望对岸的旧栏杆也在山顶；
能看见什么？泼墨的长卷不留星点的空白，
风如挽联般飘卷，惟有越织越厚的雾
从高空垂落，可以切割成枕头、床和被单，
充填在空荡如我们头脑般的房间。

黑鸟的翅膀惊起在檐头，犬吠
来自山脚的村庄；尽管关上了窗户，
仍然能够听见低吼的潮水
一浪接着一浪，就像靠岸的独木筏
催促着我们立刻出发——

the grotto

unable to trail the setting sun,
it is dark when we arrive.
the earth's turning axis squeaks between the banks,
the river seems buried in a deep cave,
only audible over the hovering horizon.

the hotel atop the hill—
a lane that once wound through bai juyi's old age,
is piled with leaves unable to return to branches;
in the hotel registration book,
we are condemned as aliens.

watching the old railings on the other bank atop the hill;
what is there to see? the long ink-splashed scroll shows
    no spot of white,
wind unrolls like an elegiac couplet, only the fog weaves thicker
and falls straight from the sky, and is cut into pillows, sheets and
    quilts,
filling up a room that is empty like our mind.

a blackbird startles on the eaves, dogs bark
from the village at the foot of the hill; though the windows are closed,
the roaring tides can still be heard
wave after a wave, like a raft pulled to shore
urging us to set off now—

今夜我们不过河,
临睡前我们仍旧打开电视,
像灯蛾依偎在冰冷、颤动的荧光,
我们宁愿石窟继续风化在对岸的夜幕深处,
一如整个历史都安睡在大自然的陵寝里。

河流标明一条心理的界线,
我们害怕地狱般的血腥和腐朽一起复活,
自己像棋盘上的卒子再无回返的机会——
却又在梦中端起微弱的烛台,走上石阶,
去瞻详遥远的黄金时代。

tonight we cannot cross the river,
at bedtime we still turn on the tv,
like moths leaning in the cold trembling light of fluorescence,
we would prefer the grotto weather deep in the night on the far bank,
like history asleep in the tomb of nature.

the river marks the limit of the psyche,
we fear that the purgatorial blood and the decay might revive,
ourselves like pawns on the chessboard who can no longer
    return—
but in a dream raise a candelabra, walk up the stairs,
and scrutinize a faraway golden age.

first appeared in Tupelo Quarterly

寄北

我梦见一街之隔有家洗衣店，
成群的洗衣机发出一阵阵低吼。
透过形同潜望镜的玻璃圆孔，
能看见不洁的衣物在经受酷刑，
它们被吸入机筒腹部的漩涡，
被吞噬、缠绕，来回翻滚于急流，
然后藻草般软垂，长长的纤维
在涌来的清水里漂浮，逐渐透明；
有一股异样的温暖从内部烘烤，
直到它皱缩如婴儿，在梦中蜷伏。
那里，我脱下那沾满灰尘的外套后
赤裸着，被投放到另一场荡涤，
亲吻和欢爱，如同一簇长满
现实的尖刺并且携带风疹的荨麻
跳动在火焰之中；我们消耗着
空气，并且只要有空气就足够了。
每一次，你就是那洗濯我的火苗，
而我就是那件传说中的火浣衫。

to the north

i dream of the laundromat a street away,
herds of washing machines roar and growl.
through the bathyscopic view of a porthole,
soiled clothes are going through tortures,
as they are sucked into the swirl of the machine belly,
devoured and snarled, twisting in torrents of water,
then sagging like sea grass, long fibers
afloat in surges of clear water, becoming more transparent;
an uncanny warmth bakes from within,
until it crimps like a baby, curls up in sleep.
there, after taking off my dusty overcoat
naked, i am thrown into another wash,
kissing and love-making, like a bush full
of reality's thorns and marked by nettle rash
sizzling in the flame; we consume
air, and having just air would be enough.
everytime around, you are the flames that wash me,
and i am the asbestos shirt that legend tells of.

first appeared in Tupelo Quarterly

江南共和国
　　——柳如是墓前

I

裁缝送来了那件朱红色的大氅，
它有雪白的羊毛翻领，帽商
送来了皮质斗笠，鞋店送来长筒靴。
门外，一匹纯黑的马备好了鞍——

我盛装，端坐在镜中，就像
即将登台的花旦，我饰演昭君，
那个出塞的人质，那个在政治的交媾里
为国家赢得喘息机会的新娘。

已是初夏，冰雪埋放在地窖中，
在往年，槐花也已经酿成了蜜。
此刻城中寂寂地，所有的城门紧闭，
只听见江潮在涌动中播放对岸的马蹄。

我盛装，将自己打扮成一个典故，
将美色搅拌进寓言，我要穿越全城，
我要走上城墙，我要打马于最前沿的江滩，
为了去激发涣散的军心。

south-of-yangtze, a republic
—before the grave of liu rushi

I

the tailor brings in the vermillion cloak,
which has a snow-white turned-out collar of fleece, the hatter
brings in a leather rain hat, the shoe shop brings in high boots.
out the door, a night-black horse already saddled—

i am dressed in my sunday best, sitting in the mirror, like
a vivacious young lady about to take the stage, in the role of
    zhaojun,
the hostage that crossed the border, the bride in political
    copulation
won a moment of breath for her country.

now early summer, ice and snow are buried in the cellar,
locust blossoms of years past have been made into honey,
this moment the city quiet, all the gates shut tight,
only the river's rolling tide broadcasts hoofbeats from the other bank.

i am dressed in my sunday best, dressed as a literary allusion,
blending allure into a parable, i want to cross the city,
i want to climb the walls, i want to horseback to the river front,
for the sake of rousing our demoralized troops.

II

我爱看那些年轻的军士们
长着绒毛的嘴唇,他们的眼神
羞怯而直白,吞咽的欲望
沿着粗大的喉结滚动,令胸膛充血,

他们远胜过我身边那些遗老,
那些乔装成高士的怨妇,
捻着天道的人质计算着个人的得失,
在大敌面前,如同在床上很快就败下阵来。

哦,我是压抑的
如同在垂老的典狱长怀抱里
长久得不到满足的妻子,借故走进
监狱的围墙内,到犯人们贪婪的目光里攫获快感,

而在我内心的深处还有
一层不敢明言的晦暗幻象
就像布伦城的妇女们期待破城的日子,
哦,腐朽糜烂的生活,它需要外部而来的重重一戳。

II

i love watching those young soldiers
and their downy lips, the look in their eyes
shy and yet frank, their hemming and hawing desires
bob within their large adam's apple, above blood-swelled chest,

they are far better than those holdovers around me,
those complaining ladies who pass for honorable men,
rubbing beads of heavenly ways to tally their own loss and gain,
before the enemy, as in bed, soon pulling back from the fray.

alas, i feel repressed
like a wife in the arms of an old warden
too long unsatisfied, on some pretext entering
the walled yard and harvests pleasures from the inmates'
    hungry gazes,

but deep in my heart there is
an obscure illusion that i dare not speak of
like the women of boulogne looking forward to the breaching
    of city walls,
alas, decadent life, it needs a hard thrust from the outside.

III

薄暮我回家,在剔亮的灯芯下,
我以那些纤微巧妙的词语,
就像以建筑物的倒影在水上
重建一座文明的七宝楼台,

再一次,骄傲和宁静
荡漾在内心,我相信
有一种深邃无法被征服,它就像
一种阴道,反过来吞噬最为强悍的男人。

我相信每一次重创、每一次打击
都是过境的飓风,然后
还将是一枝桃花摇曳在晴朗的半空,
潭水倒映苍天,琵琶声传自深巷。

III

at dusk i come home, trim the wick to burn brightly,
i use delicate and smart words,
like reflections of an edifice on the water
to rebuild a godly pagoda of humanistic culture,

once again, pride and tranquility
ripple through my heart, and i believe
there is a depth that cannot be conquered, it is like
a vagina that can swallow even the most virile men.

i believe that every deep wound, every hard blow
are passing whirlwinds, and afterward
peach flowers still waver in clear mid-air,
a pond reflecting the vast sky, sound of pipa rumbling
    from deep alleyways.

first appeared in Silk Road Review

我想起这是纳兰容若的城市

我想起这是纳兰容若的城市,
一个满族男人,汉语的神射手,
他离权力那么近,离爱情那么近,
但两者都不属于他——短促的一生
被大剧院豪华而凄清的包厢预订,
一旦他要越过围栏拥抱什么,
什么就失踪。哦,命定的旁观者,
罕见的男低音,数百年的沉寂需要他打破——
即便他远行到关山,也不是为了战斗,
而是为了将辽阔和苍凉
带回我们的诗歌。当他的笔尖
因为吮吸了夜晚的冰河而陷入停顿,
号角声中士兵们正从千万顶帐篷
吹灭灯盏。在灵魂那无尽的三更天,
任何地方都不是故乡。活着,仅仅是
一个醒着的梦。在寻常岁月的京城,
成排的琉璃瓦黯淡于煤灰,
旗杆被来自海上的风阵阵摇撼;
他宅邸的门对着潭水,墙内
珍藏一座江南的庭院,檐头的雨
带烟,垂下飘闪的珠帘,映现
这个字与字之间入定的僧侣,
这个从圆月开始一生的人,
永远在追问最初的、动人的一瞥。

it comes to me this is nalan xingde's city

it comes to me this is nalan xingde's city,
a manchu man, a sharpshooter of the chinese language,
he was so close to power, so close to love,
yet neither belonged to him—this short life
was reserved for opulent and lonely boxes in an opera house,
when he wanted to cross the railings and embrace something,
it would disappear. alas, fated witness,
rare baritone, only he could break centuries of silence—
even his journeys to border passes were not to fight battles,
but to bring back to poetry
the vastness and the desolation. when his brush-tip
fell still due to soaking in icy rivers of the night,
soldiers in a myriad tents were snuffing lamps
amid bugle calls. in the endless third watch of the soul,
nowhere was home. living, merely for the sake
of a waking dream. in uneventful years in the capital,
rows of glazed roof-tiles faded in soot,
flagstaffs shook in sea wind;
the door to his mansion faced a pond, inside the walls
he treasured a courtyard from south-of-yangtze, rain from the eaves
was wreathed in smoke, gleaming bead curtains swayed to reveal
a monk sitting quiet between words,
a man whose life began from a full moon,
always questing for that first moving glance.

Poems by Han Bo 韩博诗选

大卫 • 佩里英译 Translations by David Perry

韩博，1973年生于中国黑龙江省牡丹江市。诗人，戏剧编剧、导演，旅行作家，艺术家。1991年至1999年，先后就读于复旦大学国际政治系与新闻学院。2009成为美国爱荷华大学荣誉作家。出版有中文个人诗集《借深心》（2007年作家出版社）、《飞去来寺》（2013年台湾秀威）等，诗歌作品被译为多种文字，在美英法德出版。曾获刘丽安诗歌奖（1998）和诗东西PEW诗歌奖（2012），曾参加2009年美国爱荷华大学国际写作计划、2010年大陆诗人访问台湾交流活动、2014年法国巴黎第37届英法诗歌节和2015年德国第十六届柏林国际诗歌节。

HAN Bo, born in Heilongjiang in 1973, is a poet, journalist, essayist and playwright. He earned an MA in Journalism from Fudan University in Shanghai. He was editor-in-chief of the travel magazine mg (2000-2007), the Chinese version of the Swedish magazine Rodeo (2008-2009) and the weekly magazine Channel Young Pictorial (2009-2013). He has published several collections of poetry. He attended the International Writers Workshop in Iowa in 2009. He was awarded Liu Li'an Poetry Prize (1998) and *Poetry East West* Poetry Prize (2012).

中东铁路（2011）
黑龙江-内蒙古-上海

现代性器

当代：有时，她
住在临时里。现代
是格林尼治时间
擒住的铁轨，着急，
茶汤咬盏。有时，
她强拆人造的现代，
她住在自焚念头
的当代里：黑烟甩
向俄国，进步的
等死之物无从拆起。

（2011/7/3 上海）

The Chinese Eastern Railway (2011)
Heilongjiang – Inner Mongolia – Shanghai

Modernity Tool

Contemporary: Now and then, she
lives within the momentary. Modern times
mean Greenwich Mean Time
lives lived caught on the tracks, anxiety,
tea foam nipping at its bowls' walls. Now and then,
she demolishes man-made modern times,
she lives within the self-immolation of the thought
of the contemporary: black smoke pours
toward Russia, progress's
waiting-to-die substance cannot be demolished.

(2011/7/3 Shanghai)

红军街

哈尔滨:人流喧沸,煮肥白昼。
火车搬来的俄国已被俄国的学生
吃光,多余的黑夜,通电,携手
霓虹与斯大林伪造学生的俄国。

吃不起白昼的诗人只好白吃等待,
等待是卷饼,薄薄的乡村母亲,
裹紧来路不明嗔荤怨素的父亲,
霓虹与斯大林伪造的煮肥的等待

吃空诗人的半生,多余的卷饼
裹紧平庸:平庸不分行,白昼的
平庸增肥三十小时,时间的轮刑
等待脱轨的火车搬来别的等待。

(2011/6/18 哈尔滨;2011/7/12 上海)

Red Army Street

Harbin: crowds boil with commotion, the day's crackling fat.
The trains have rendered White to Red, Russia devoured
its own students, night rendered superfluous by electricity,
    hand-in-hand
neon and Stalin stamping out forged students of Russia.

Unable to afford to eat that day the poet had no choice but wait,
wait for a half-eaten egg wrapped in its juǎn bǐng, the wrapped-up
    old country mother
in from who-knows-where, the bitterly cursing old father,
neon and Stalin stamping out forged waiting-time's crackling fat

for the poet half a lifetime of eating next to nothing, a half-eaten
    juǎn bǐng
offhandedly wrapped: offhandedness does not distinguish, the white
    day's
offhandedness fattened by thirty hours, time's next round of
    punishment
waiting for a derailed train to depart en route to yet more waiting.

(2011/6/18 Harbin; 7/12/2011 Shanghai)

野鸭与磕头机

车窗：默念湍急。
平原的湍急，野鸭
下蛋的季节，磕头机
与王进喜默念时不我与。

冻土保温的如画的热的闷墙
湍急：火车捉轨，火车捉鬼。

车窗：将来湍急。
将来：匮乏时代的
车窗：愤怒解决方案。

季节驯育的野鸭
只为湍急的平静下蛋。
石油的平静从未歇脚。

车过大庆，鬼撞心的乘客
庆幸野鸭：无心的逃票者，
彼此乱投彼此，时不我与。

(2011/6/18 哈尔滨至满洲里；2011/7/15 上海)

Wild Ducks and Kowtow Machines

Train windows: contemplation's rapid flow.
The marshy plains' channels flow, wild ducks
lay their eggs in season, crude oil pumpjacks
together with Wáng Jìnxǐ kowtowing contemplating time
without me.

Frozen earth sealed off by heated insulated walls picturesque
waters rushing past: the train picks up speed, the train picks up
    ghosts.

Train windows: the future's rapid flow.
The future: the deficiency of the time's
train windows: anger settling on a plan.

Wild duck breeding season yields
eggs laid amidst the rapid flow's tranquility.
The tranquility of oil never-ending.

Passing through Daqing, ghosts knock up against paying
passengers' hearts
wild ducks take flight: fare-dodgers ride black
taking refuge among one another, time without me.

(2011/6/18 Harbin to Manchuria; 2011/7/15 Shanghai)

黑烟挂晒

道为天下裂,黑烟
挂晒:卧轨唤醒沉睡
的浩然无足采信。

大地从未沉睡,梦游
只为蜂出的黑烟挂晒。

内燃机的怜悯梦见
丘原:旱草枯对
牛羊,粪便与泥尿
冷而油腻,大地
挂晒的污迹跃动
而感染捷径。

像骑马人的牙齿一样松朽,
像夜空挂晒眼神一样失眠。

怜悯挂晒,巡视夏的表层。
车厢里的进口意志梦见
草的主人下马,定居
水泥潮闷的汉语;牛羊
的夏啃光骨瘦的鼠灾。

黑烟为天下裂,只身
打马:打马的铁轨的
使者假托高速而不动。

(2011/6/19 满洲里;2011/7/18 上海)

Hung Out to Dry in Black Smoke

The way the road splits all beneath Heaven: in black smoke
hung out to dry: strewn across the tracks to awaken
some slumbering sublimity, lying beyond all belief.

The earth never sleeps, yet sleepwalks
like bees rising into black smoke.

The internal combustion engine's compassion dreams
of ancient fells: hay stuck
to cattle and sheep, feces, mud and urine
cold and grease-caked, the earth's
smoke-stained filth teeming
with disease vectors.

The horseman's teeth like rotting pine,
The look of insomnia like eyes hung out to dry in night skies.

Pity the hanging sun, patrolling summer's surface.
From his chariot's driven dream of power and will
the master of the plains dismounts, settles
into cement-choked Chineseness; cattle and sheep
wasting away summer-long bone-thin amidst a plague of rats.

Black smoke splits all beneath Heaven, alone
on horseback the emissary rides the rails
pretending at high speeds to be remaining still.

(2011/6/19 Manzhouli; 2011/7/18 Shanghai)

大地离合

汽笛吹干前朝，吹干
日凿一窍的混沌，耳目
口鼻的鲜湿各有变速，
地址经伪制各有激奋：

绥芬河，绥阳，绥西，太岭，红房子，马桥河，下城子，穆棱，牡丹江，一面坡，玉泉，阿城，哈尔滨，万乐，肇东，安达，让湖路，喇嘛甸，泰康，昂昂溪，富拉尔基，龙江，碾子山，成吉思汗，扎兰屯，巴林，博克图，免渡河，牙克石，大雁，海拉尔，大良，乌固诺尔，乌兰丘，东宫，完工，都伦，陵丘，赫尔洪得，皇德，豪门，嵯岗，湖北，扎赉诺尔，扎赉诺尔西，东壕，胪滨，满洲里。

（2011/6/18 哈尔滨至满洲里；2011/7/18 上海）

Shifting Earth

The steam whistle blasts the previous dynasty dry, blasts
Hundun's primordial chaos dry, bores holes through the day,
eyes and ears
mouth and nose fresh and oozing every time the gears shift,
each station enduring its makeshift forgery with every violent
push:

Suifenhe Station, Suiyang, Suixi, Tai Ridge, Red House, Ma Qiahe,
Xia Chengzi, Muling, Mudanjiang, Yimainpo, Yuquan, A Cheng,
Harbin, Wanle, Zhaodong, Anda Lake Road, Lamadian, Taikang,
Angangxi, Fùlāěrjī, Longjiang, Nianzishan, Genghis Khan,
Zhalantun, Balin, Boketu, Miandu Ford, Yakeshi, Wild Goose,
Hailar, Daliang, Uzernal, Ulanqiu, East Temple, Wangong, Du
Lun, Ling Qiu, He'er, Hongde, Huangde, Haomen, Cuogang,
Hubei, Zhalai Norr, Zhalai Nori West, East Gulley, Lubin,
Manchuria.

(2011/6/18 Ha'erbin to Manzhouli;2011/7/18 Shanghai)

持续的,断续的

餐车里,随你揣度的人
感激脚踩风火轮的集体:
集体晃荡,集体不承平,
不着制服的菩萨不腥熟。

站着吃面条的人,感激
制服制不服的一切:你
看,草原快进的黎明白,
土豆猪肉左右集体堆壁。

制服:持续地女与好。
麻袋:断续地男的难。

(2011/7/22 上海)

The Steady-going, the Broken Off

In the dining car, you might think the people would be
grateful for the wind of Nezha's fiery wheel at the collective's feet:
the collective wobbling, the collective lack of peace,
un-uniformed bodhisattvas, nothing fishy here.

People standing to eat noodles, grateful
for all that joins in refusing uniforms: look,
see the grasslands fast-forwarding to daybreak,
meat and potatoes piling high to form collective walls.

A proper uniform: a steady woman playing nice.
A burlap sack: a broken man breaking bad.

(2011/7/22 Shanghai)

时间的卧铺

平躺着：快到了，快到了。

梦直立，像约会，像合同：
松针，婚戒，松昏的嘴角
悬而未决一线垂涎：半生
穿过诺言又回垂成的半生。

下车，上车，俄国穿过
内蒙古黑龙江又回俄国。
下车，每一座丢失时间
的小站杜撰土地的半生。

汽笛松昏，从未去过俄国
的时间离家又回家，卑微
平躺着：快到了，快到了。

（2011/6/20 满洲里；2011/7/18 上海）

Sleeper Time

Peacefully reclining: almost there, almost there.

Dreaming vertically, like a meeting, like a contract:
pine needles, wedding rings, a blurred slack mouth
hanging open strung with drool: half a life
passing promises that break up into halved lives.

Off-board, on-board, boring into Russia
Inner Mongolia Heilongjiang and back again to Russia.
Off-board, every seat takes up time
at every local station making up lost ground for half another
lifetime.

The steam whistle dies down, never making it to Russian time
leaving home again and returning, reduced to
peacefully reclining: almost there, almost there.

(2011/6/20 Manzhouli;2011/7/18 Shanghai)

新县城

天气预报说服天气，
现实服从主义：麋鹿
服从迷路。雷阵雨
的塑料袋摔向身后的
中转站，新县城像
半盒剩饭，嘘地一声
加醋添油。主义的
速度肿胀：卸下大同，
运走旧社会与不同。

郊野间，天气失眠：
铁轨抽送的复印机
未留空处，浅睡的
偶尔已被塑料袋里
游泳的人推搡挤占。

隐士进城，自比废纸篓：
暗箱盛凶吉，运命各殊悬。
废纸失眠，复印大同的
失眠无法复印无为或同治。

塑料袋里上岸的佛陀，
脱下自比泳装的
内裤：松紧带深耕
赘肉的勒痕：旧村镇
唯一存储过往之地。

（2011/6/20 满洲里；2011/8/5 上海）

New District

The weather report persuades the weather
to obey reality's ideology: the red deer
obeys the maze of deer trails. Thundershowers
hurl plastic bags to earth in back
of the transfer station, the new district resembling
half a box of leftover food, hissing exhalations
add vinegar and oil. The ideology of
rapid swelling: do away with Datong, the Great Community,
ship off the old society and assemble the new and different.

Suburban fields, insomnia weather:
train rails pumping it out photocopiers
leaving no space to live, light sleep
often sometimes already occupied by plastic bags
swimming with people, shoving, pushing back, seizing ground.

The hermit heads into the city, compares himself to a
wastepaper basket:
a camera obscura containing the unlucky, each and every fate
suspended within.
Wastepaper insomnia, to copy Datong's
insomnia is to be unable to copy wuwei or perhaps even the
Tongzhi Emperor.

Washed ashore in a plastic bag Buddha
sheds his swimsuit really
it's just underwear: the elastic band's bitten deep
into his fat impressing its mark: the old villages
the sole ground of memories come and gone.

(2011/6/20 Manzhouli; 2011/8/5 Shanghai)

大杀器

蒸汽自西天来，
蒸汽手挽云的剪纸
觉民行道：晕车，农妇
攥紧钱袋与零存整取的半生的汗的畏途。

道不远人，农妇与马蒂斯
都爱剪纸，饥乱交剪丰静而贴天上人间。

（2011/8/8 上海）

Mass-Murder Tool

Steam from the Western Paradise,
steam a hand cutting out paper-cut clouds
awaken the people on their way in the street: motion-sick, a peasant woman
clutches her purse with nothing to show for half a lifetime of sweat and hard roads.

The way never abandons the people, the peasant woman and Matisse alike
love to make paper-cuts from both hungry chaos and bountiful calm and
    paste them Heaven and Earth.

(2011/8/8 Shanghai)

POEMS BY MING DI 明迪诗选

Translations by Ming Di except otherwise specified

明迪，出版有《明迪诗选》、《和弦分解》、《几乎所有的天使都有翅膀以及一些奇怪的嗜好》，之前独立出版《D小调练习曲》《柏林故事》《日子在胶片上流过》，在美国出版《分身术》《长干行》，另有西译诗集《碎月》《分心》，法译诗集《家谱》《七命书》《创世》。兼文学翻译，出版有《在他乡写作》《错过的时光》《舞在敖德萨》《家》，合译《仙鹤丛书》《空椅子》《三语连诗》《新华夏集：当代中国诗选》等，以及沃尔科特纪录片的中文翻译（荷兰出版）。2016年与墨西哥诗人合编《中国新诗百年孤独》。目前编辑《鹏程：中国新诗100首》（英语/印地语）。

Ming Di is a Chinese poet, translator and editor living between California and Beijing, author of six collections of poetry. Her work appeared in the national prestigious "Chinese Poetry One Hundred Years Canon" (Yangtzi River Arts And Literature Publishing House, 2013). She has translated four books of poetry into Chinese, and edited and co-translated four books of poetry from Chinese into English including *New Cathay - Contemporary Chinese Poetry* (Tupelo Press 2013) and *Empty Chairs* (Graywolf Press 2015, finalist for the Best Translated Book Award in 2016). She co-edited (with Alí Calderón) *Una soledad de cien anos Nueva poesia china 1916-2016* (One Hundred Years Solitude of Chinese New Poetry) (Valparaíso Ediciones México, 2016). She has received translation awards and fellowships from the Poetry Foundation and Henry Luce Foundation.

寻找玛雅

> 姐姐玛雅失踪的地方
> 土地分裂成海洋和岛屿

从前有一朵巨大的云。
父亲挥手切成天和地。
从前地上有风和尘。
母亲把灰尘捏成人。
要有光。于是有了光。
要有字。于是有了花朵字,
石头字。从前花朵上飞出一条鱼
飞在天空和地球间。
从前鱼嘴里飞出一个太阳。又一个太阳。
又一个太阳。又一个太阳。石头变成动物
不能忍受太阳的热。
于是父亲踢足球,踢走太阳,
留下一个,在空中讲故事。从前有个故事,
玛雅姐姐和我在岩石上刻字,竹子上刻字,
棉花和丝绸结绳记事。
她喜欢给花朵画齿,给鱼鸟画足。
所有的生物都有翅膀,飞来飞去,
她想让他们留在地上。
于是地震,土地分裂,
分裂成大陆和岛屿。
我看见她越漂越远,直到一个海洋
横隔我们之间。

Looking for Maya

> Where you disappeared, Sister Maya,
> the land split into oceans and islands

Once upon a time, there was a huge cloud.
Father waved his hand and cut the cloud into sky and earth.
Once upon earth, there was just dust.
Mother shaped the dust into humans.
Let there be light. There came the light.
Let there be words. There came the words
of flowers and stones. Once upon a flower, a fish came out
flying between the sky and earth.
Once upon a fish, a sun came out. Another sun.
Another sun. Another sun. The stones turned into animals
that couldn't bear the heat of the suns.
Father kicked out the suns like kicking footballs,
leaving one in the sky to tell the stories. Once upon a story,
Sister Maya and I carved picture words on rocks, bamboos,
and made string words with cottons and silks.
She liked to draw teeth in the flowers, and feet
for the fish and birds. All the creatures had wings flying
but she wanted them to stay
on earth. Then came an earthquake that split the land
into continents and islands.
I saw her drift away further and further until there was an
ocean
between us.

几千年飞过山，几千年飞过水，
文字让我苟且不朽。
我去日本找她，看到很多相似的字，但她不在。
我去马来西亚，印度尼西亚，菲律宾，夏威夷，
太平洋的岛屿都有她的痕迹，
直到我来到复活节岛，从那里到达智利
和秘鲁。我在秘鲁留下线索让她找我。
我向北移，最后在危地马拉和墨西哥，
我看到她的后裔在洞穴和贫民窟。他们遗失了
她的花鸟字。
他们用罗马字母书写。
他们谈论诗歌，仿佛诗歌始于西班牙。他们忽略
自己的口述历史和古代文字。
玛雅姐姐死了。
我的一半死了。"闭嘴，"一个声音从加勒比海
传来，"讲你自己的故事。"
是的，先生，这就是我的故事。
我是中国人，苏美尔人，埃及人，非洲人，祖鲁人，
玛雅人，爱斯基摩人，萨米人，切诺基人，纳瓦霍人，
圣卢西亚人，我要么什么也不是，
要么是鸟，鱼，天空，海洋，彩虹，雨，雨林，风，
所有**风物**于一身。

Years and years have drifted away but the words we share
make me immortal.
I go to Japan and see many similar words but she is not there.
I go to Malaya, Indonesia, Philippines, and Hawaii
and all the islands in the Pacific and see many traces
until I land on Easter Island, and from there I reach
Chile and Peru. I leave strings for her to find me.
I move north, and finally in Guatemala and Mexico
I see her descendants in caves and slums. They have lost
her words, the words of flowers and birds.
They write in the Roman alphabet.
They talk about poetry as if it started in Spain. They ignore
the oral history and ancient writing.
Sister Maya is dead.
Half of me is dead. "Shut up," a voice from the Caribbean
says, "tell your own story." Yes Sir,
this is my own story.
I'm Mayan, Sumerian, Chinese, Taiwanese, Zulu, Inuit,
Sami, Cherokee, Egyptian, St. Lucian…
and I'm either nobody or I'm
bird fish sky ocean wind cloud rain rainbow all in one body.

黄花鱼和松香草

芸芸，云云，转身听见鸟语
飞翔，飞向
他乡。鸟在他乡筑巢
如同我把手搭在眉眼就是屋檐

她走过雪覆盖的草地
我仿佛看见自己冰川期来过这里
旧石器时代来过这里
农耕时代又来过这里，仅仅是长高了一点
她对着冰海祈祷，我读她的唇语
才知道要么是她要么是我，进化
无法再回到海底

松香草在夏天，开出黄色的花朵
形状，颜色，都像太阳
但不是菊花，如同我不是向日葵
也有黄色的血液，我仅仅是面朝太阳
就拥有了太阳的肤色，如同当初
仅仅是看见松香，就放弃了海洋
心里想着太阳，就长出了翅膀

这个季节的草都是单性繁殖
这个季节的花都有太阳的光谱色
这个季节的鸟都悬在半空
这个季节的鱼只有花黄鱼
还保留原始的姿势

Yellow Flower Fish and Rosinweeds

Clouds... Crowds... You make a turn and hear
birds—that fly—fly toward a
foreign land. Birds nest anywhere as I
put my hand above my eyebrows to make an eave.

She walks on the snow-covered grass.
I seem to see myself arriving here in the ice age,
arriving again in the old stone age
and again in the farming age. A little taller each time.
She prays before the frozen sea. And I read her lips
knowing that either she or I have evolved
unable to return to the seabed.

In the summer time, rosinweeds grow yellow flowers
that smell like rosin, same color as the sun.
They are not chrysanthemums, as I am not a sunflower,
but have sun-yellow blood. I just face the sun
to take on the sun's color, as in the past
I just breathed in the rosin to give up the sea.
I thought of the sun and grew wings.

This season, all grass and weeds are self-reproducing,
all flowers pale in the spectral color of the sun,
and all birds hanging in midair.
Only the yellow flower fish, the croakers,
maintain their prehistorical elegance.

所有的生物都源自太阳
放射出的光，甚至水果，不同的波长
他说我肤色浅，我说你是黄花鱼
后代，而不自知，你的眼睛
是东方的形状。古时候一直向东游
就游到了西方，上岸，点火

我们争吵，而记住了对方的嘴型
如同一个神秘的字母
一个新的符号系统。玉米黄，柿子黄，桔黄……

唇齿留香的，柠檬黄
甚至连海水也不过是一次点缀

All creatures are made from sunlight,
even fruits, in different wavelengths. He sees me
as having lighter skin than him. I say
you are an offspring of yellow fish. Your eyes oriental.
In ancient times, one could keep swimming east
to reach the West. Then, landing on the shore, start a fire.

We argue and remember the shape of each other's lip.
A mysterious O. A brand new symbol system.
Yellow corn, yellow persimmons, yellow oranges…

What stays on our lips is the scent of yellow lemons,
even the sea fades away.

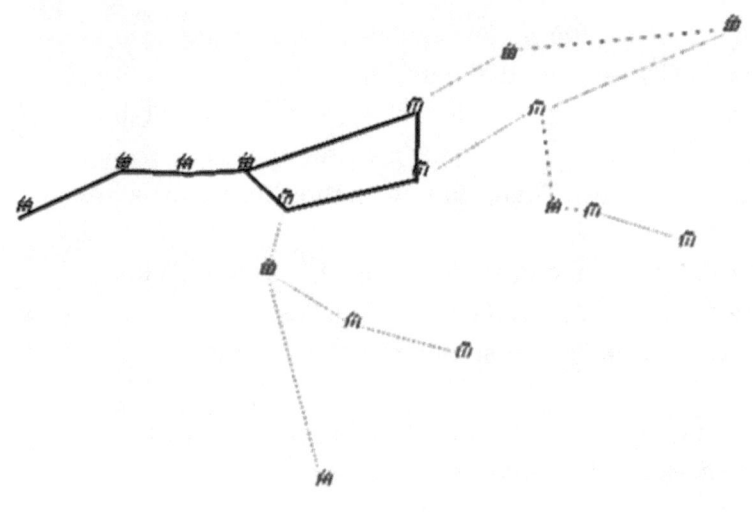

海叶集

从水的方向看,海是一棵树
鱼,是海里的风吹动叶

你说你和他风水不合,一个属天
一个属地,一个信教,一个对教水土不服

教为何物我不知,出于孝,你走之后我每夜观天
看星象,二十五年了很多鱼

飞上天,有些掉下来,有些留驻,双翅合十
最坚定的那一批,合成了北斗星

如果你低头看我的眼睛,你会看见更多的星
栖息于我的视网膜——它们是一些有痛感的树

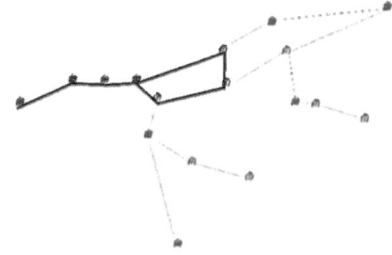

Sea Leaf

The sea is a tree
and the fish, the fish are leaves
that waft in the water.

Mother—she belongs to the sky
and my father, she says, to the earth
as she's a believer,
and he, she says—is not.

From where I was born, Hubei, China,
I don't know what it is
to be a believer but I see many fish fly

toward the sky
each night. Some fall back
to the earth, some stay there longer.
The firm ones form a Big Bear that brightens
the April night.

But look down, Mother, look into my eyes,
you'll see many more stars—
they're trees, trigger points of pain
on my retinas.

Zeeloof

De zee is een boom, en de vissen -
de vissen zijn loof
zwevend in het water.

Moeder - zij hoort bij de hemel
en mijn vader, zegt ze, bij de aarde
want zij gelooft,
zegt ze, en hij - niet.

Vanuit mijn vaderland China
heb ik geen weet van wat het is,
gelovig te zijn - maar 's nachts zie ik

vele vissen vliegen naar de hemel omhoog.
Er zijn er die terugvallen op aarde, er zijn er
die langer boven blijven. De sterkste
vormen een Grote Beer, schittering
in de aprilnacht.

Maar kijk omlaag, Moeder, kijk in mijn ogen,
daar zie je nog veel meer sterren -
bomen zijn het, priemende punten van pijn
op mijn netvlies.

Dutch translation by Anneke Brassinga

The image of Sealeaf is the Big Bear Constellation in characters of fish 鱼, the tails connecting the stars.

Memorial Song 清明之歌

Mound to cloud, my mouth open
sings. I must
or you will miss what I'm missing.

My voice a curved line: 3 5 6 5 i- 7 • 6 5 6 5 3 - - -

Atop the rice heap—we hear
mother's deep-sing.

My song
a bell's throat
through murmuring air. Past moon

and lotus—a starry belt—
you clear
the mist, and I—a new moon, barely risen—
approach the void and barren.
My fall into a square word cages me;

```
ㅁㅁㅁㅁㅁㅁㅁㅁ
ㅁ              ㅁ
ㅁ              ㅁ
ㅁ    人       ㅁ
ㅁ              ㅁ
ㅁ              ㅁ
ㅁㅁㅁㅁㅁㅁㅁㅁ
```

each word's square mouth, calling without
tongue or tooth.
I must sing a square song—
hear me,

I covet words;
the wing-squared cage,

each square-cloud-cage compels my lungs
to breathe a stricken bird.

```
            ⌺
         ⌺
      ⌺
ㅁ
ㅁ                ㅁ
ㅁ    人        ㅁ
ㅁ                ㅁ
ㅁ                ㅁ
ㅁㅁㅁㅁㅁㅁㅁㅁ
```

风 Feng

I give birth on a water lily

a string of tunneled echoings,
my belated children's song:

*Atop the rice heap—we hear
mother's deep-sing.*

Water lilies to many lotuses;
in each pinhole the moon falls deaf
to other ears.

This morning I see rain.
I know it's you—or snow, snow—
I see you fall,
covering.

My aged eyes open but you —
you are still young
like April.

Notes:
The images in the original Chinese poem are made using the characters below.

口 means "mouth" or "opening." A tilted ⟁ resembles a cloud and/or mound.

人 means "human." When tilted, 亻 resembles a bird in flight.

囚 means "encaged" or "imprisoned." The word is made of a mouth 口 and a human 人.

Translated by Michael Benedetto with Ming Di
First appeared in *Peotry International* (USA)

Cat 猫

Pat's always asking for a cat, but I can't even
put her up, where would I put Pat and a cat?
So Pat draws herself as a cat on the wall.
One day the cat meows. Pat jumps up, puts
on a hat made of a cat, runs out and

falls on her hat. Another meow from the
wall. Another cat. Like a cat confused, I chase
Pat and her cat-hat. I nearly catch her when I
hear Pat's cries from the house. I run
back like a scared cat to look for Pat, and
find only

a cat on the wall wearing Pat's cat-hat.
I scream, "Where are you, Pat?!"
I often dream like this, afraid
to wake up as a nameless cat with no
language. Just meeeeooowws.

I meow to another me, the cat that is always
missing,
Like a rat chasing a cat.

Translated by Carolann Madden and Ming Di

一片树叶能说出什么

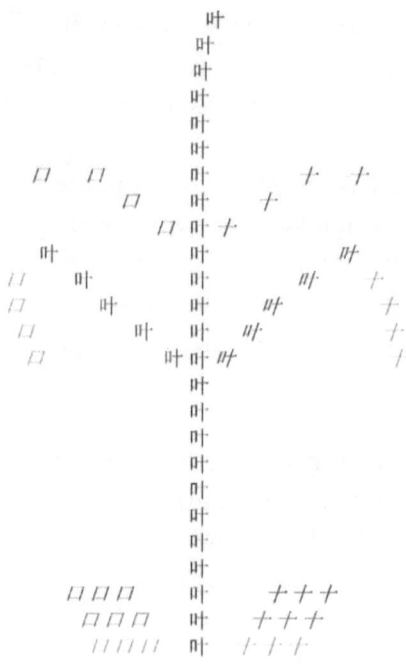

天问在风中敲打
白杨树,答案枝离叶碎——
一千片白色的叶子
一千张无辜的口
一千种白色的口实
我拾起一片
握紧
如同拥有一整棵树
屈原说一片树叶
确实
比一棵树
能说出更多关于树的真相
而唐人说一片树叶
可以道出 整个秋天的秘密
我却只看到一片树叶
一片树叶

叶 leaf or leaves
The image is a deconstruction of leaves. The character "leaf" is made of two parts, mouth 口 and ten 十. *Kou* 口 is a component of *jiekou* (excuse) and *koushi* (evidence); *shi* (十) is a pun with *shi* (truth) in Chinese.

What One Leaf Tells

In the wind, questions to heaven bang
the white poplar. Answers fracture—

a thousand white leaves. A thousand
blameless mouths. A thousand. Ten
thousand colorless excuses;

I pick one up. Grip tightly
as though holding the whole

tree. Indeed, Qu Yuan says the leaf,
more than the tree, tells the truth
about the tree. Indeed, Tang people

say the leaf lays bare great secrets
of autumn. But all I see is one leaf.

Translated by Carolann Madden and Ming Di
First appeared in *World Literatue Today* (USA)

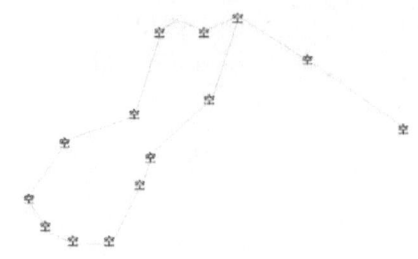

水瓶·座

水瓶座是一个美男子,面相年轻,
身体是一只老鹰。
开始他很自在,村里人一多,他便披一件黑大褂,
低飞。
冬天到了,风吹起黑大褂,人们发现他走路时脚不着地。
"巫!""杀死他!"于是他飞走了。
但每天傍晚,人们发现空中有一只乌鸟,
然后,天很快就黑了。
人们花一夜的时间,终于把乌鸟赶走。但每天傍晚他都飞来,
仿佛把魂留在了村里。
于是全村人集合,抓鬼。但没有一个人
承认。长老说,天黑之前若没人承认,就全部杀光。
这时一个白衣女子,从人群里走出,
甩一下衣袖,长裙,飞上天去。
乌鸟不相信自己的灵魂
或者灵魂伴侣是一个女子,吹出一口气。
等他看清时,一条河已形成。

每年七七,乌鸟飞过河去见她
爱上她,或者爱过就忘。
他来来去去,寻找什么。
寻找什么他并不知道。

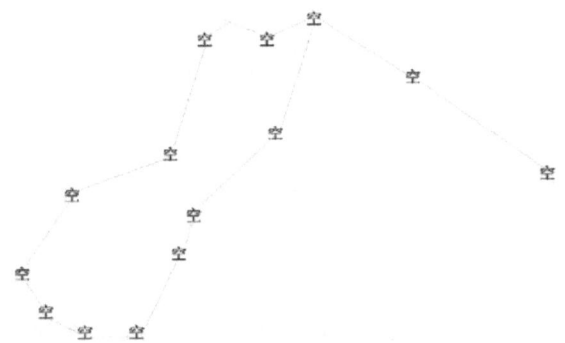

Aquarius

Aquarius is a handsome man, his face young, human,
his body an old eagle.
In the beginning he's at ease. When people appear in the village,
he puts on a black coat, flying low.
Winter comes. Wind blows up the black coat,
people see him walk with his feet not touching the ground.
"Witchman!" "Kill him!" He flies away.
But every day at twilight, people see a black bird in the sky,
then it's soon dark.
People chase the black bird away. But he returns every dusk
as if he has left his soul in the village.
Villagers gather, try to find his soul, but no one admits.
The elder man says, if before dark nobody admits, all will be killed.
Then, a woman in a white dress comes out,
swinging her sleeves and dress, and flies up.
The black bird doesn't believe his soul or soulmate is a woman.
He blows air.
When he sees clearly, a river is formed.

Once a year on July 7th he crosses the river, meets her,
falls in love, and out.
He comes and goes. Searching for something.
Or nothing.

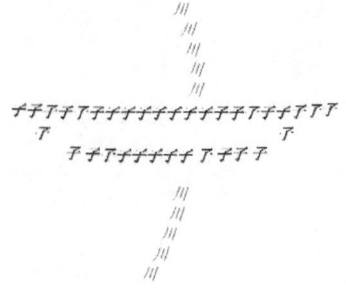

Image: Confucius speaks on the stream

船

是秋天的落叶
外星人穿过的鞋子
是月亮

是天海一线，飞鸟栖息
是燕子
是水上走散的星辰

是未能抵达彼岸的虹
留下的翅膀
是书签，把我和另我分开

是星移斗转七千里
太阳在深夜刻舟
求的那把剑

是清晨我家门前的小溪
流过
一只香蕉皮

```
              /1/
              /1/
              /1/
               /1/
                /1/
 千千丁千丁千千千千千千千千千千千丁千丁 丁 丁
   丁                            丁
       千 千丁千千千千 丁 千丁 千
                /1/
                /1/
                /1/
               /1/
              /1/
```

Boat

It's a leaf falling in the Fall.
A shoe an alien has worn.
A moon.

A wandering star.
A bird flying down the azure sky.
A sparrow.

It's the wing of a rainbow
that couldn't reach the other shore.
A bookmark that cuts me from the other me.

It's the sword that the sun is searching
after it's fallen into the stream
seven thousand miles away.

It's a banana peel
that floats in the water before me
at this quiet moment.

清明叨念

我让词语伸展四肢,你才能辨识

从你的方向看过来,所有的黑字如同蚂蚁
所以我必须让我的蚂蚁飞起来
舞动四肢

而我每动一次就会伤到你
而蚂蚁自己飞舞
而你每天死去

十岁时母亲说她死后上天
父亲死后下地

我不知道天地之间是大爱小恨,还是
小爱大恨,还是大小不分
爱恨不分

天地崩裂后,地上只有安静
如同相安时,心里只有心静

有一天我从母亲的眼睛里醒来,看见地面上
词语,张牙舞爪

只有一个字,张开,如同一把太阳伞

Nagging@memorialday.com

I stretch my words like limbs
that you might notice them.

In your eyes, mother, all words a crawl
of ink-wet ants. My ants swarm and dance, so you
will see me in these roiling insects,

but I hurt you with my outstretched hands.
And now, their daily strut and sway
is tuned in time with your mortality.

When I was ten, you told me you would die
and go to heaven; father, down to earth.

Between the two, what flies each way?
Immensity of love, a sigh of hate,
or all reversed?
Or no change in size and shape—
no difference between love and hatred—
no difference between love and love?

When the sky and earth crack open—only peace,
as in peace, lives a slivered calm.

One morning I awake half deaf, mother,
while with their violent claws,
the mute words shout.

But quiet, like a sun umbrella, one word opens out.

Translated by Michael Benedetto with Ming Di

爻 *yin yang* in the Book of *I Ching*, or simply 4 lines

四月·九歌

四月是四个翅膀的月亮梳着中分
上弦下弦
同时开花
四月是四只眼睛死死对着，从河的一边
对到河的另一边天就亮了
四月是天亮后月亮下
雨
下进我眼睛，直到月亮在河水里

四月是我看不清一朵莲花
冰上革命
垂柳，青丝，白发香草
四月是雏菊
是盲点，是我看不清任何别的人
或神

四月是木棉
是大雁
是飞舞，飞翔，飞向
是安静地躺下
是山坡
是草地
是堆满箱子的房间
是一盏灯
亮了通宵，是我
从你眼中醒来你从月亮中坐起
是开河
是吹箫
是声烟袅袅，危机四伏

April, Nine Songs

April is a four-winged moon with hair
parted in the middle: waxing and waning,
two crescents blooming.
Four eyes locked into each other's
move from this shore to the other shore
of the river, then day breaks.
April is the rain from the moon. It rains
into my eyes
and rains till the moon sets in the river.

April is a lotus flower that I can't see
through. A coup d'état on the ice,
willows weeping. Black hair. Gray-haired beauty.
April is a daisy,
a blind spot in the center. I can't see other people
or gods.

April is a kapok tree,
a wild-goose
flying, dancing, wandering,
and then nestling quietly.
April is a hillside.
Grass.
A room full of boxes.
A lamp
lit all night. I awake from
your eyes when you rise from the moon.
Ice breaks, splashing.
A flute quivers, its sound winding
up the hill, crises hidden in four corners.

汉字神话学

> 我是我的语言抛下的身影
> ——帕斯

星星每天老去,你还是年轻的,萨拉,
我每小时老去,我的文字还是年轻的,
很多最后的探戈,只差一步
我们就相遇了,但我终究还是要离开的。
昨晚我梦见你把我身体切割,重新组装
成一些怪字。汉字会变成那样吗,萨拉?
两千年以后,真的会像树叶一样在空中飘?
人们说话只需摘下几片叶子?那么下雨代表什么?
下雪代表什么?狂风骤雨代表什么?
我将怎样表示还没有爱够?相爱或者毁灭?

五千年前一个极度抑郁的流窜犯,每日狂书,
刺在龟壳上,然后用自己的头发上吊,
死在半空中。风把他吹回你的星座,
他呛一口水活过来,回头看地球:
龟壳闪闪发亮,夜不能寐,上面的字伸展肢体,
呈飞翔状。五千年后,它们在纸上舞蹈,
随意组合,乱伦,难以忍受与生具来的渴望和孤独
它们被绑架到银屏上,肢体扭曲,伤痛,
有声,有形。气温变了,故乡消失,
网络窒息,它们每天跳楼自杀,
剩下的那些偏旁部首,象不象形,会不会意,形不形声,
谁去在意。每一个字都是一只鸟,像人一样行走,
纠结,残杀,它们是自己上吊的鞋带。*

Modern Mythology of My Language

I am the shadow my words cast.—Octavio Paz

Stars grow old each day, you are still young, Sarah.
I'm growing old each hour, but my words stay young.
There are many last tangos, por una cabeza. With one step
missing, we have almost met. But I would have left
in the end. Last night I dreamed of you cutting me apart,
reassembling my body into strange characters.
You think Chinese will look like that, Sarah?
In two thousand years, words will fly around like leaves?
People would just pick up a leaf to speak?
What would rain stand for? What does snow mean?
What does a thunderstorm try to say? What would I do
to say I have not loved enough? Love more or perish?

Five thousand years ago, a depressed outlaw carved words
on turtle shells, and then hanged himself with his hair.
Dead in the air. Wind blew him back to your constellation.
He choked on a mouthful of water and woke up. He looked back
at the Earth: the turtle blinked and glittered, unable to sleep,
words dancing on it, stretching limbs, ready to fly.
Five thousand years later, now, they dance on paper,
making free combinations as if in adultery.

Unbearable desires and loneliness born with them, in them.
They are kidnapped onto computer screens, their bodies
distorted, in painful sound and images. Climate changes,
homeland disappears, internet suffocating.
They jump from skyscrapers. Daily suicide.
The remaining pictograms or ideograms, phonetic or not,
who cares. Each word is a bird, walking like a human.
They tangle, strangle, killing each other. Each stroke a string,
to hang on it or to hang itself.

Image: a self-made character of water and light, meaning light
walks on the stream. But the strokes, the light beams, look like
hair or strings. Sarah is the who hanged herself with her shoe
lace.

* 萨拉·凯恩（1971 – 1999）为英国90年代新文本运动剧作家，有《摧毁》《菲德拉的爱》《清洗》《渴望》《4点48分精神崩溃》五个剧本，1999年以鞋带上吊自尽。

POEMS BY SONG LIN 宋琳诗选

李栋英译 Translations by Dong Li

宋琳，1959 年生于福建厦门，1983 年毕业于上海华东师范大学中文系。1991 年移居法国，曾就读于巴黎第七大学远东系，先后在新加坡、阿根廷居留。2003 年以来受聘于国内几所大学执教。目前专事写作与绘画。著有诗集、随笔集多部，其中《断片与骊歌》（法国ＭＥＥＴ出版社，2006）、《城墙与落日》（法国巴黎Caractères出版社，2007）为中法双语版；编有诗选《空白练习曲》（合作，牛津大学出版社，2002）。《今天》文学杂志的诗歌编辑，《读诗》主编之一，《当代国际诗坛》编委。曾获得鹿特丹国际诗歌节奖、《上海文学》奖等。

SONG Lin, born in Xiamen, holds a literature degree from East China Normal University. He has published five collections of poetry (two of which were translated into French and published in France), two books of prose, and has co-edited a contemporary poetry anthology. He is the poetry editor of the journal Jintian [Today]. Among his honors are Rotterdam, Romanian, Hong Kong Poetry Night International Poetry Fellowships as well as the Shanghai Literature Prize. He has held residencies at OMI Ledig House translation lab and Vermont Studio Center.

遗 忘

1
日晷。头颅。谁退藏于密?
谁的仪表画出虚妄的圆弧?
你眼睛的祭坛深陷着
在未来某个庞大建筑的对面

彗星落向木樨地时
倘若我是你,你或许就是他:一个尾数
她最后的回首穿过了
呦呦鹿鸣

2
雪的谐音喷涌
花,无痛地绽放
一朵催开了死亡的非花
是真的。它攀上了你的名字

痉挛的灌木下
道具般的脚趾涂着萤火虫的黑盐
也是这么被抬走了
像极了新近地震中的场面

Forgetting

1.
The sundial   heads   that receded in secret.
Whose metre drew out their false curves?
The altar of your eyes was sunken
facing an immense building of tomorrow

when a comet hit muxidi1.
If I were you, you could be him: a mantissa
her last glance crossed
the bellowing of the deer.

2.
The red homonym of snow, spewing
flowers, blooming painlessly
a flower triggered the opening non-flower of death
which was real. It climbed onto your name

under shrubs in spasm –
prop-like toes were painted in the black salt of fireflies
and were carried away like this
very much like the scenes of the recent earthquake.

3

喷枪那闪电节奏的火舌
吻遍娇嫩的脸。清晨的水龙头
把夜的灰烬灌溉了又灌溉
结痂的将长成石笋,在心脏部位

一个失踪者走来,一个失踪太久的
失踪者,瘦长的手臂像唐·吉诃德
读秒的时间到了。你来读,像秒针一样读
履带的嘎嘎声里是什么已对峙了千年?

3.

Lightning-fast flames from the machine guns
kissed every tender face. The morning taps
washed over and over night's ashes
the scabs would turn into stalagmites, in the heart

a missing person came by, a person missing
for too long, his thin arms looking like Don Quixote's
countdown time was up. Please read, read like the second hand
    of the clock
in the rattling of tracks, what has been mired in confrontation
    for a thousand years?

1 An important access point into central Beijing from the west suburbs. On June 4 1989 the greatest number of casualties occurred here.

first appeared in Asia Literary Review

西湖的晴和雨

塔中的舍利在夜晚放光,在白天
说着箴言:摆渡的人正打开一扇水之门!
曾经是禁苑的内湖泄漏了春色,
馈赠午后一场短暂的晴雨交合。

从波心吹来蚕与蛾的思乡曲,
太阳在云中吐丝,在水面织网,
我在你眼睛里垂钓红鲤鱼,
上岸来呀,快接住这个耀眼的词。

湖畔派坐着痛饮杯中的虹霓,
当风把堤上接踵的游人熏得睡着了,
苏小小就从墓里出来,唱一曲:
云破处,销魂雨过,犹恨晴晚。

The Sun and Rain of West Lake

The Buddhist relics in the stupa shine at night. During the day
they read the saying: The ferryman is opening a gate of water!
The once-forbidden inner lake now leaks spring light
with the gift of a brief afternoon play of sun and rain.

From the rippling middle blows the homesick song of silkworms
and moths –
the sun spits threads in the clouds and weaves nets on the
    water.
I fish the red carp in your eyes –
come ashore to hold fast this dazzling word.

The lake poets sit and drink up rainbows in the glass.
When wind smokes wave after wave of visitors to sleep,
Su Xiaoxiao comes out of the grave and sings:
where the clouds break, ecstasy after the rain, sigh for the late sun.

黄昏把西湖磨成最耀眼的词，
丁香在你的发绺间窃窃私语，窃窃私语，
你眼睛里的鱼游入我的怀中，
我取出一封信，我升上孤山顶眺望你——

岸柳像那祝英台恢复了女儿身，
披一袭青烟的婚纱飘向夜，
你的莲藕心结在水上，你投胎为人，
领我穿过每一处秘闱重阁。

Twilight grinds West Lake into the most dazzling word
lilacs whisper in your tresses; whispering,
the stream of fish in your eyes swims into my arms.
I take out a letter, I rise to the solitary summit to watch you –

like Zhu Yingtai, the willows by the bank put back on their
maiden clothes
and in a wedding dress of blue smoke, drift to night.
Your lotus heart grows on the water, you reincarnate as a
   woman
and take me through every pavilion and every secret quarter.

Note: Su Xiaoxiao was a legendary courtesan who lived during the Southern and Northern Dynasties and was buried by the West Lake.

first appeared in Asia Literary Review

城墙与落日
——给朱朱

在自己的土地上漫游是多么不同，
不必为了知识而考古。你和我
走在城墙下。东郊，一间凉亭，
几只鸟，分享了这个重逢的下午。

轩廊外的塔，怀抱箜篌的女人，
秦淮河的泊船隐入六朝的浮华。
从九十九间半房的一个窗口，
太阳的火焰苍白地驶过。

微雨，行人，我注视泥泞的街，
自行车流上空有燕子宛转的口技，
雾的红马轻踏屋顶的蓝瓦，
我沉吟用紫金命名了一座山的人。

湖，倒影波动的形态难以描述，
诗歌一样赤裸，接近于零。
对面的事物互为镜子，交谈的饮者，
伸手触摸的是滚烫的山河。

我用全部的感官呼吸二月，
我品尝南京就像品尝一枚橘子。
回来，风吹衣裳，在日暮的城墙下，
快步走向一树新雨的梅花。

City Walls and Sunset
—For Zhu Zhu

How different it is to roam in our own land,
no need of archeology for the mere knowledge. You and I
walk by the city walls. In the eastern suburb, a pavilion,
a few birds, an afternoon together shared of reunion.

Pagodas seen beyond lofty galleries, a lady holds in arms an ancient harp,
on the Qinhuai river moored boats fade into fleeting glories of six dynasties.
A window from ninety-nine inner chambers,
sunflames palely drive through.

Drizzles, passers-by, I stare at the muddy street,
above a river of bicycles, the ventriloquist swallow turns,
red horse of fog treads softly on the roof of blue tiles,
I muse on the person who named a mountain Purple Gold.

A lake, wavering patterns of its reflection difficult to describe,
naked like poetry, close to zero.
Opposite things mirror each other, drinkers in a conversation,
rivers and mountains burning close to the touch.

I breathe second moon of the year with all my organs,
I taste Nanjing as if tasting an orange.
Upon return, wind through clothes, by the city walls in sunset,
I sprint to a plum tree of blossoms in a fresh rain.

first appeared in PEN America

临近

　　酒的乡愁。一支歌。无所事事烦闷的回忆。是什么隔离了我与遥远？蓦然回首中漂浮的是归乡之路的幻影吗？鹤，飞越虚空的冰。

　　如果故园不野蛮，异乡不会有更多漫游者。但我们不知道天气的阴晦原本来自万古愁的遗传。过去即未来。我们种姓象征中的巨龙在贪欲喧器声中被更大的贪欲所驯服。麒麟的独角、凤凰的美冠早已随崩溃的礼乐灰飞烟灭了。世界贫血地凸现在它那火山与洪水的双重影像中，废墟裸露末日之美。

　　诗人，将你遭放逐的声音注入遗忘的颅腔，既不太迟，也不太早。"解放"是对被缚者最原始的祝福。除非用酒温暖骨头，我们以泪水为粮食的日子还嫌不够悠长？酒跳出鹤的机舱，为我们打开落向无地的降落伞。

　　悬而未决从日子那边向我们临近了，星空与恐惧临近了。我在一个停顿与下一个停顿之间，如被光芒扔在遗忘之河上的浮标。远离，克制，活着就是与死亡对饮。

Near

Homesick of wine. A song. Ennui, anguished reminiscence. What separates me from the faraway? Looking back on a whim, is it the mirage of the way home that wavers in the mind? Crane, the ice that flies through the void.

Should our homeland be not barbaric, there would not be more wanderers. But we do not know that the dim weather inherits sorrows from the long-gone forevers. The past is the future. In the noise of greed, the giant dragon that symbolizes our race becomes tamed by the ever-greater greed. The unicorn horn, the phoenix crown have long vanished into thin smoke as music and mores crumbled to ashes. The world bloodlessly emerges in the double image of volcano and flood, as ruins expose beauty of the doomsday.

Dear poet, pour your exiled voice into the long forgotten cranial cavity, nor too late, nor too early. "Liberation," an ancient blessing for the oppressed. Unless we warm our bones with wine, aren't the days unbearably long when we take tears for food? Wine jumps off the crane cabin and opens for us a parachute to the groundless void.

From the days dangling and now nears us, starry sky and terror near. I stand between this break and the next breaking, as if a buoy left on the river by light. Separation, restraint, living is to drink with death.

first appeared in PEN America

缓缓登上心之山巅

修远——在浓云后面,光
之瀑泻下。井,摇柄如桨,咕噜噜
把渴意泼进瀚海的咽喉、瀚海的眼睛
白杨树,孤零零一棵,承受过天斧

隳突的路,没有路,只有上下与南北
寥廓惚恍的寂寞。没有虹,只有海市的皮影
一盏油灯点在石窟里。朝圣的躯体褴褛
他灵魂的手杖,丈量着修远

slow climb to the summit of heart

long and winding—behind thick clouds, the light
cascades. the well, crank like oar, water grunting
thirst sloshed into throat and eyes of vast ocean
a poplar singly stands, a ragged road
that has withstood the heavenly

ax, no road, only up and down south and north, wandering
vast loneliness. no rainbow in the sky, only mirage of shadows
a kerosene lamp lit in the grotto, a pilgrim's body in tatters
the cane of his soul measures this long winding, this journeying

first appeared in PEN America

漂泊状态的隐喻

十二座一模一样的桥上,
没有哪一座不是车水马龙。

晚钟震响,众鸟敛迹,
尖顶隐入灰暗的天空。

目光茫然,风中最后的树叶
颤抖着,不知落向何处。

强烈感觉到分裂的自我,
仿佛十二座桥上都站着你。

听着风中的赞美诗,
置身于一片熊熊火海。

那时大雪的伞兵还在集结,
灵魂的飞蛾已劈开教堂的烛焰,

炽然超升,成为空气与黑暗。
风在桥上哭喊。那是谁的灵魂?

成为你自己,而不是别人的灵魂,
星星一样寒冷,孤独。

在车辆的尘嚣和肉体的庆典中,
成为河流,带走无言的哀愁。

塔上的圣人又怎样了呢?
空空的眼睛望入宇宙。

他脚边的怪兽那耷拉下的翅膀,
遮住了瞬间的天堂和地狱。

漂泊的雪覆盖漂泊者的大地,
树的疤痕,你自我的印迹,多么刺目。

Metaphor of the Floating Life

On the twelve identical bridges,
not a single one without endless streams of traffic.

Evening bell tolled, birds retrieved their shadows,
steeples faded into a grey sky.

Eyes in a daze, last leaves in wind
kept trembling, not knowing where to fall.

A spurt of feelings of the divided self,
as if you stood on every one of the twelve bridges.

Listening to praise songs on wind,
you were in an ocean of raging fire.

Paratroopers of the heavy snow still gathering then,
moths of the soul chopped open candlelight of the church,

rising up intensely, they became air and darkness.
The wind cried out on the bridge, whose soul was that?

Become yourself, not the soul of another person,
cold and lonely like stars.

In the bustle of traffic and celebration of the flesh,
become a river, washing away silent sorrows.

What about the saint in the pagoda?
Hollowed eyes saw into the universe.

Drooping wings of the little monster by his feet,
covered heaven and hell in a flash.

Floating snow blanketed the land of the wanderers,
tree scars, your own traces, so glaring and glaring.

first appeared in PEN America

语言简史

既无名称亦无目光,从未有过酣畅淋漓的流动
——冰川宝蓝色的沉睡。寒冬严峻的刻刀
在那透明的棺椁表面继续跳着透明的死亡舞蹈。

语言抵达那片缓坡,在昨天的猛犸离去之后。
那边走来一个穿桦皮衣的人,他有着从地狱归来的
但丁一样苍白的面容。他缓缓吐出一个词——"花"。

a brief history of language

not a name not a line of sight, never a thorough run of water
—slumbers of the turquoise icebergs. a severe wintry graver
dances still a transparent dance of death on the transparent coffin surface.

arrival of language at that soft slope, after yesterday's mammoths left.
there comes a man in a birch bark coat, wearing a Dantesque pale face
as if returning from the netherworld. slowly he blurts a word out—"flower."

first published in PEN America

无题

一枝连翘上
秋天痉挛
异乡人走过河岸
回忆使他变成一个灵魂
高大的秋天,一阵风
把落叶的黄金播入了阁楼
你的夜晚与某个天使搏斗
直到星星变成骨头

白昼之钟赤裸着
一个推迟的约会将你召唤
于是你穿过广场
松树之蓝环绕着古塔
鸟疾飞时
水上写着禁止:
石头的面容闪耀谦逊
痛苦的青苔
无语之舌

untitled

on a forsythia
autumn shudders
a stranger walks past the river bank
reminiscence turns him into a ghost
towering autumn, a gust of wind
tosses gold of leaves into the garret
your evening battles with a certain angel
until stars become bones

the clock of day naked
a belated meeting beckons
so you cross the square
blue of pine trees around ancient pagodas
no written on the water:
face of stone glows modesty
lichen in pain
wordless tongue

采撷者之诗

1

用山鹬的方言呼唤着跑出房子
蓝浆果里的声音我还能听见
雷达站,木轮车,童年的山冈
整个夏天我们都在寻找
坡地开阔而平缓,死者的瓮
半埋着。荒凉的词,仿佛涂上了蜜
我们的乐园向南倾斜,金丝雀飞去飞来
那时还没有特洛伊,我们总是躺着眺望
村庄,水杉高大,像山海经中的
有外乡来的筑路工留下的斧痕
"他闯祸,必不得其死",老人们说
而我们笑,躲在咒语中摇晃镜子

冬天拨着火炭,夏天就去后山
采撷,坐在树上等待父亲
廊桥消失了,仿佛被突降的暴雨卷走
这是既没有开始也没有结束的地方
人们只是绕着那几棵水杉树走
在历法中生活。狐狸尖叫,大雾
追着我们跑。长途车从海边爬上来
没有父亲,我们踢着小石子回家
夜里我梦遗了。哟,大捧的浆果

记得吗?那两个发亮的音节,
把我们变成蓝鬼。甚至风也变蓝了
野孩子唱道:"雷达兵,天上的雷达兵"
直到中秋的月亮升起,木轮车滑下去
浆果碎了,像伤口流出的血,仿佛为了
让我日后的手稿点染上那种蓝

the gleaner song

1.

calling out in a partridge's dialect while running out of the house
i could hear a voice in the blueberries
radar station, wooden carriage, childhood hillocks
we had been looking all summer
the slopes open and smooth, the urn of the dead
half buried. bleak words, as if dipped in honey
our paradise slanted to the south, the canaries flying about
there was no troy then, we always lay down and watched
the village, the tall fir tree, like in classics of mountains and seas
there were ax marks left by the construction workers from another town
"no good end for a trouble-maker," the elderly said
and we laughed, hiding in the curse, swinging a mirror

i flicked embers in winter and went to the mountains in summer
gleaning, sat in the tree waiting for father
the bridge disappeared, as if washed away by a summer storm
this was a place with no beginning nor end
people just walked around a few fir trees
and lived in their calendars. a fox screeched, a heavy fog
chased after us. a long-distance bus climbed up from the seaside
without father, we kicked broken rocks around and came home
at night i had a wet dream. ah, armfuls of berries

do you remember? those two bright syllables
turned us into blue ghosts. even the wind also blued
a wild children's song: "radar soldier, radar soldier from the sky"
until the moon rose in mid-autumn, the wooden carriage slid
berries crushed, as if blood from a wound, as if to dye
my manuscripts so that they read with that kind of blue

2

蒙德格伊街。儿子惊呼:"Myrtille"
新上市的浆果摆在货架上。恋人抱吻
晒成棕色的皮肤散发着海藻的气味
假期已结束。地中海留给了墓园守望人
我们避开沙滩营帐,为兽迹所吸引
迷失于山毛榉林中。我想去触摸
高地上的赛壬石,最终表明
那冲动是虚妄的,她或许死于雪崩
像树上的娃娃鱼。而传说活在舌尖

我们都喜欢这南部山区的夏季
村道垂直在门前,花荫遮住窗台
去湖边散步的人回来了
拿着新采的野菊。群峰渐次明亮
畜水池含情脉脉,屋顶更柔和
倒影中的停云像洗衣妇回眸的样子
对山,牛铃丁丁。儿子蹲在灌木丛中
四岁之夏,不知道中文名字的来由
他吃 Myrtille 这个词,抬头看见
滑翔机像风筝,轻轻越过瀑布

我的头晕症消失了,字典带来
新的苦恼。我们元素中的土生长着
同样的植物,那些枝条本是为了
纪念死者。当我们带回的自制果浆
早餐时涂上乡村面包,我将用什么解释
乌饭与寒食,以及丧失的祭天之礼?
一种凝聚的寂静深入到这里
柔软、微热的泥土,款待着我
今天我们又去登山,但选择了另一条路

2.

rue montorgueil. my son exclaimed: "blueberry"
fresh berries were on the shelves. lovers kissed and embraced
tanned skins emitted smell of seaweeds.
vacation was already over. the mediterranean left to the grave watchmen
we avoided beach tents and were drawn by animal tracks
and lost in the beech forest. i wanted to touch
the siren rock on the high ground, but eventually
the urge was false, perhaps she died in an avalanche of snow
like the giant salamander in the tree. and legend lived on the tip of tongue

we all liked summer in the southern mountains
country paths lay vertically by our doorsteps, flowers shaded the balcony
those who went for a walk by the lake came back
with freshly-picked wild chrysanthemums. mountain peaks lit one by one
the reservoir tender with feelings, the roof ever so softer, the
lingering clouds
in water's reflection looked like a washing woman turning around
in the opposite mountains, cattle bells resounded. my son squatted
in the shrubbery, his summer at the age of four, not knowing
the origin of his chinese name, he ate the word blueberry, and
looked up
and saw a glider, like a kite, which swiftly passed the waterfalls

my headache was gone, the dictionary brought in
new trouble. in the earth of our bodily elements
the same plants grew, whose branches were there
for the dead. when we put the homemade jam that we spread
on the country bread at breakfast, how could we explain
black rice and cold food, and the lost rituals of worshipping god
of heaven
a concentrated quietude deepened
into the soft and barely warm earth and served me
today we were to climb the mountain but chose another path

POEMS BY YANG XIAOBIN 杨小滨诗选

莫恺英译 Translations by Canaan Morse

杨小滨生于上海，复旦大学毕业，耶鲁大学博士。现任台湾中研院文哲所研究员，政治大学教授，《两岸诗》总编辑。著有诗集《穿越阳光地带》、《景色与情节》、《为女太阳干杯》、《杨小滨诗X3》（《女世界》、《多谈点主义》、《指南录·自修课》）、《到海巢去：杨小滨诗选》等，论著《否定的美学》、《历史与修辞》、《中国后现代》、《语言的放逐》、《迷宫·杂耍·乱弹》、《无调性文化瞬间》、《感性的形式》、《欲望与绝爽》等。近年在两岸各地举办个展"涂抹与踪迹"等，并出版观念艺术与抽象诗集《踪迹与涂抹》。

YANG Xiaobin was born in Shanghai, holds a PhD from Yale and currently works as a research fellow at Academia Sinica in Taipei. He has published several books of poetry and poetry criticism. He won the First Poetry Book Prize in Taiwan and has served as jury member for international literary committees. His abstract photography along with abstract poetry has been exhibited in Taipei, Shanghai and Beijing titled "Palimpsest and Trace: Post-Photographism."

为女太阳干杯

不过,当太阳蹲下来嘘嘘的时候,
我才发现她是女的。

她从一清早就活泼异常。
树梢上跳跳,窗户上舔舔,有如
一个刚出教养所的少年犯。

她浑身发烫。她好像在找水喝。
我递给她一杯男冰啤:
"你发烧了,降降温吧。"

她反手掐住我脖子不放:
"别废话,那你先喝了这口。"
她一边吮吸我,一边吐出昨夜的黑。

"好,那我们干了这杯。"

瞬间,她把大海一口吸干,醉倒在地平线上:
"世界软软的,真拿他没办法。"

Toasting the Female Sun

However, it wasn't until the sun squatted to pee
that I realized it was female.

She had been unusually peppy all morning.
She hopped about on branches, and licked the windows, like
a juvenile offender just released from detention.

She burned all over. She seemed to want a drink of water.
I passed her a glass of male beer, ice-cold:

"You have a fever. This will lower your temperature."
She easily caught hold of my neck and gripped hard:

"Stop babbling. You have some first."
She sucked me dry, while blowing out last night's black.

"All right. Let's finish this glass."

She drained the ocean in one gulp, and fell drunk on the horizon.
"The earth is so soft. There's nothing I can do about him."

电子游戏

一

你逃脱的时候,另一个逃亡者开始了
他的旅程。你们相背而逃

另一个你在屏幕前告诫:
请把生命关掉!

逃在赴死的快乐里,你的
不知名的敌手的鲜艳
其丑无比的天空也湛蓝起来

好象梦的果汁一瞬间就泼掉
来不及喝干,就倾倒在血浆里

好象风驰电掣的血比你更焦急
另一些敌手跳跃在你的脚步里

你们相遇了。就是这倒霉的时刻
你在电源面前犹豫不决

Video Games

1.

As you escape, another fugitive begins
his travels. You run in opposite directions

Another you in front of a screen cautions:
Please turn off your life!

Fleeing inside a euphoria headed for death, your
nameless enemy's vibrant colors
an incredibly ugly sky drains into bright blue

It seems that a dream's fruit juice is spilled all at once
no time to drink it all, pour it right into plasma

It seems that blitzkrieg blood is more impatient than you are
Some other enemies leap within your footsteps

You meet. It's at this unfortunate moment
you vacillate in front of the power outlet

二

射杀鸭子，和晚餐一样简洁。
猎人在猎艳的过程中误伤鸭子
他的枪转向影子的过程。
因为鸭子本来也就可以没有。

所有的蹼都被枪声的调味所腐败。

临死时的悦耳，夏日的枪声
谁来倾听？谁记得来埋葬？

闪电被击中，它的羽毛
一泻如注。好象思春的少女
爱上湖里的自己。

2.

Shooting ducks is as clean and simple as dinner.
The hunter of words accidentally injures a duck

The process of his gun's turning toward a shadow.
Because ducks can always be done without.

Every toe-web is corrupted by the gunshots' seasoning

Aural reverie before death, gunshots on summer days
Who will listen closely? Who'll remember to bury them?

Lightning is hit, its feathers
fall off like water. It appears a lovelorn young girl
has fallen for her own reflection in a lake.

三

宝藏和我们,分不出彼此。
为了那些吃不完的金子
睡不完的木乃伊

明天的晨铃今晚就响起!
令人激动的门在头脑之外闪耀:
这是陷井的、幽闭的美。

是水晶,还是头颅
会把我们带向终点?

门在头脑之外,钥匙藏在灵魂深处。
一片永远打不开的灵魂
坟墓在生前就已掘好。
空的坟墓,无人租用。

而尸首躺在锁孔中,千年不动。

3.

We and treasure are indistinguishable from one another.
All for more gold than one could eat
more mummies than one could sleep

Tomorrow's morning bell rings tonight!
The door that excites people shimmers outside the skull:
this is a booby-trapped, cloistered beauty.

Is it crystals, or heads
that will take us to the last stop?

The door is outside the skull, the key hidden deep in the soul.
Space of eternally unopenable soul
its tomb was dug while it still lived
an empty tomb, no tenants residing

But the body lies in a keyhole, untouched for a millennium.

四

从刀里出来，就一头扎进拳头
那个脸色惨淡，目不暇接的人
他用无限的恐怖挣扎

那个石头般的人，敲得粉碎！
一路上的花，纷纷刺眼
那个人惊险，那个人春寒料峭
比起我们，他更加虚构
时时自己看不见自己，他用眼泪
烫伤了自己！

从午夜出来，又被白昼捆住
那个人情不自禁地喊叫
"……！"他
紧紧握住空气，紧紧地奔跑！

他的衣裳在鸟的追逐中
他的脊背在鸟的啜泣中

他的影子痛如刀绞。那个无始无终的人
一直死到不能再死

4.

He came from a knife, dove right into a fist
this man with a drained face that's more than the eyes can take in
He grapples using an unlimited fear

That stone-skinned man is knocked into powder!
The flowers along the way pepper the eyes with pain
That man is dangerous, that man is February chill
Compared to us, he's more fictitious
frequently can't see himself, he burns
himself with tears!

Straight from midnight, snared immediately by day
the man can't resist shouting:
"…" He tightly
grips the air, tightly runs away

His garments are in the birds' pursuit
His spine is in the birds' whimpers

His shadow hurts like a twisted blade.
That beginningless and endless man
keeps dying until he can die no further

信件·面包·书签（三首）

信件

午餐之前，你听见信封里的叫喊。
你把它打开：一封
寄自本埠的情书，落款是
小夜曲。

你坚持把它封死。就象
埋掉一只夜莺。你怕

那首歌。你把它扔回邮筒
直到第二天
它又在你的信箱里呻吟

面包

你用梳子切开面包。那里
有死者的发丝，娇嗔
烤热的爱。

面包越来越黑，碎屑
越来越理不清：

梳洗之前，你的脸已烧焦。
难以下咽的五官
带着美的饥饿。

Letters • Bread • Bookmarks

LETTERS

Before lunch, you hear shouting in an envelope.
You open it: a love letter
sent by local post, the signature saying
Nocturne.

You resolve to seal it shut. Like
burying a nightingale. You fear

that song. You throw it back in the post bin
until the next day, when
it's whining again in your mailbox

BREAD

You slice bread with a comb. Here is
the hair of the dead, love baked
in coquetry, still warm.

The bread gets blacker, crumbs
harder to organize:

Your face is burned black before you've washed.
Your sensory organs stick in your throat.
They carry a beautiful hunger.

书签

你打开一本尘封已久的书:
一只手
夹在书签的位置。

它不愿意离开,它死死地
抓住这个字
一个句号。

枯萎的手,书页上的化石
等待另一只手的掌声

BOOKMARK

You open a dust-covered book:
a hand
holds a bookmark's place.

It will not leave, it stubbornly
grips this word
one period.

Desiccated hand, this page-born fossil
awaits another hand's clapping

左翼文人似是而非的环球旅行

往左,再往左。我就来到右边。
但环绕了大地,岁月飞逝。

是否能更迅捷?比如,一转身
右边的同行者就站到了左边。

目光与时间相悖,旅行者,我,
与酒徒相悖,与家的飞翔逆向

往前:泪水的流程、血的飞溅
还是往上:越过另一个世纪的塔尖俯视?

灿烂的,必然是单向的。在
天亮的时辰回头,比起在黄昏

追逐落日更容易错?但一次旅行
能同时抵达两个以上的终点吗?

一个是乏味的天堂,另一个
比地狱更痛,比革命更高潮?

旅行者,我们,在史前地图上向
另一个昼夜,左冲右突……

为了节省时间,我们把中国扔进美国。
消失的是起点。旅行者剩下了未竟的旅行。

The Left-Wing Writers' Spurious Global Tour

Turn left, then left again. I arrive on the right.
But I've circled the whole earth, as years have vanished.

Could I be more expedient? For example, I turn around
and the traveler on my right now stands on my left.

Gaze and time contradict, travelers, drunks,
and I contradict, moving against home's flight path

Go forward – tears' procedure, blood's spatter
or go up – pass over the spires of another century and look down?

What glitters can only be one-way. Is it
easier to make mistakes looking back during the dawn hours

than chasing the sun at dusk? But can one journey
finish at two destinations at once?

One a flavorless heaven, the other
more painful than Hell, more orgasmic than Revolution?

The travelers, we, are charging and elbowing our way
on prehistory's map toward different days and nights…

To save time, we pitch China into America. What disappears
Is the point of origin. Travelers are left with a trip untaken.

燕尾蝶
——给臧棣

终于可以数清身上的燕尾蝶了。
就像嘴唇不是纹身，蝶衣
也有如一醉方休的粉刺
在一阵咕咕之后又开始沙沙。

虽然风不如口哨靓丽，还是有细雨
掉进午夜里，让幸福变得更忧愁。
再这样下去，连尘暴都要带上京城口音了，
根本不理会喷嚏里的春天和声学。

要眩晕几次才能让发梢的舞姿停下？
或者在山巅盘旋，还能闻到鱼的鲜美？
今夜，樱花咬碎了耳朵——
巧的是，睡莲也吮破了手指。

Swallowtail Butterflies
for Zang Di

At last I can count all the swallowtail butterflies
on my body. Just as lips are not tattoos, those wings
have drink-till-you-drop pimples that coo
before they start to rustle.

Though wind isn't as foxy as whistling, fine rains
will still drop into midnight, making happiness more worried.
If it continues this way, even sandstorms will pick up Beijing accents,
and completely ignore the springtime and acoustics
in a sneeze.

How many dizzy spells does it take to halt the hair's dance poses?
Or to stand on a summit and catch whiffs of fish-freshness?
Tonight, cherry blossoms chew up their ears –
by coincidence, water lilies also bit their fingers.

后拳头主义

把一座岛捏在拳头里
说不准扔向哪里。
拳头是长在手上的鸟。

惊弓,顺便也惊世
拳头笑起来,吓坏了宠物狗。
天气好得暗藏暴风雨。

全身喇叭开花,唱清香,
拳头鼓咚咚,迎来新节日。
并肩躺到晴天的怀抱。

披挂了鲜艳,简直
认不出旧爱新欢。
脸谱换了好几个朝代,
依然只说自己最美。

那么,借一顿别人的拳头,
才能趁热捶打镜中的胸膛。

拳头飞起,不知所终:
本世纪一具性感幽浮。

Postfistism

Squeeze an island in your fist
There's no telling where you'll toss it.
That fist is a bird grown on the wrist.

Gun-shy. Might as well be globe-shy
Fists burst into laughter, scaring a domestic dog.
The weather's so good, it hides a hurricane.

Morning glories bloom all over the body, singing a fresh scent
Balled fists drumroll, ringing in a new holiday.
They lie side-by-side in the arms of a clear day.

So girded with gaudy color, you can barely tell
Old flame and new fetish apart.
Though their painted masks switch for several dynasties,
They still say they're the most beautiful.

Thus you borrow a beating of someone else's fists
before you can strike the chest in the mirror while the iron's hot.

Fists fly forth to an unknown end:
This century's sexy UFO.

假春天主义歌谣

街上绿得发慌,邮车
送来坏消息就走。
暖风里有无限懒意,
养肥了我们的好胃口。

满眼滑溜溜的云,
告诉我们天是容易逃走的。
楼顶全都被鸟喊尖
还刺不破季节的谎言。

阴雨甜腻了太久,
连闺蜜们也荡漾起来,
一边晕车,一边唱高音。

激情处,张开就是艳丽。
但她们吹出的不是花粉,
是过期的美白霜。

Song for Faux Spring-ism

The streets are uncomfortably green. The mail truck
Delivers bad news and runs away.
A warm breeze bears unlimited laziness;
It fattened up our healthy appetite.

Sky full of slippery-slick clouds
Tells us that heaven can easily escape.
Though rooftops have all been screamed sharp by birds,
they still can't puncture the season's lies.

Fine rains have been cloyingly sweet for so long,
Even bosom sisters are feeling restless,
Getting carsick as they sing soprano.

At climax, every opening is glamour.
They aren't puffing out pollen,
But expired whitening cream.

未来追忆指南

那时候,我还活着,也还没
烧掉滚滚浓烟的胡须,
我自比狮子,走在钢索上。

直到有一天,我从梦中坠下,
风吹远了我的双耳——
谁都看成是蝴蝶扑飞,
幸运的是,那不是死后的爱。

比乌云更重的我,果然
飘不起来,也抓不住
风的任何一对翅膀。

那时候,雨下个不停,
我还年轻,山上树也都还绿着,
我以为我真的很有力气,
但我举不起曾经的时间。

A Guide to Recollecting the Future

In those days, I still lived. I hadn't burned out
the black, rolling smoke of my beard.
I styled myself a lion, walking a steel wire.

Until one day, I dropped out of my dream,
And the wind blew off my two ears –
Everybody thought they were a flapping butterfly
Luckily, that wasn't love after death.

Heavier than storm clouds, I really
Couldn't float, nor could I catch a single pair
of the wind's wings.

In those days, it just kept raining.
I was still young, the trees on the mountain still green;
I really thought I was very strong,
Yet I couldn't lift time that had once been.

旧社会指南

我去旧社会,其实是为了
找个军阀喝杯酒。假如时间宽裕,
就顺便买场饥荒来瘦瘦身。

当然,最好参观下满目疮痍,
在恶霸横行时揭竿而起
也会是一次不错的历险。

我去旧社会,还有
骗女繁体字谈个恋爱的小心思。
要不,穿件破马褂,
拍一拍末代的雕花女栏杆?

这一去,我就很难回来了。
因为旧社会太旧,
是价值连城的真古董。而新社会
不过就是旧社会的山寨版。

Guide to the Old Society

I'm going to the Old Society, in fact,
to find a warlord to drink with. If time allows,
I'll buy a famine on the way to slim me down.

Of course, I really should go visit the endless devastation;
to rise in revolt when vicious tyrants rule
would be a fairly exciting trip.

I'm also going because I have
half a mind to trick female Chinese characters into dating me.
Or, shall I put on a threadbare robe,
and snap pictures of a fin-de-siècle carved female banister?

Once I go, returning will be difficult.
The Old Society is so old, it's made of real antiques
worth more than cities, while the New Society
is merely the pirated version of the Old.

POEMS BY ZANG DI 臧棣诗选

English Translations by June Snow

臧棣出生于北京，北大毕业，现任教北大中文系。出版诗集《燕园纪事》（1998）、《风吹草动》（2000）、《新鲜的荆棘》（2002）、《宇宙是扁的》（2008）、《空城计》（2009）、《未名湖》（2010）、《慧根丛书》（2011）、《小挽歌丛书》（2012）、《骑手和豆浆》（2015）。曾获珠江国际诗歌节大奖（2007年）、《南方文坛》杂志2005年度批评家奖、第3届珠江国际诗歌节·诗歌大奖（2007）、第7届华语文学传媒大奖·2008年度诗人奖（2009）、首届苏曼殊诗歌奖（2010）、首届北京文艺网国际华文诗歌奖（2013）等。

ZANG Di was born in Beijing and has been teaching Chinese literature at Beijing University since 1996. He has published ten collections of poetry. He was a visiting professor in the US in 1999-2000 and 2009, and in Japan in 2006 and 2012. He has been the chief editor of *Chinese Poetry Review* and other independent journals. As one of the most original and proliferative poets in contemporary China, he has won many national literary awards including "The Critic of the Year" (2005), Ten Best Young Poets (2005), Ten Best Poets (2006), Ten Best Critics (2007), First Literary Award from Yangtze Literature (2008), "Poet of the Year" from the Media Chinese International (2009), first Su Manshu Poetry Award (2010), and Poetry Award from the Arts Beijing (2013).

夏天的对峙

这里,从前要用沙漠来说明的事
现在,用蚂蚁就可以挑明。

此刻,蚂蚁停止了黑色的忙碌,
全都懒散在天使竖起的中指上。

你也许看错了人,但必须承认
你始终都没看错世界。

半个月前,你就想邀请一只蚂蚁
进入夏天的诗歌。

现在事情进展得很顺利,
简直像在拍电影。而主要情节

也确实完美得如同一条伟大的线索:
你,正与一只蚂蚁对峙在大象的孤独中。

1998.7.

Summer Confrontation

Here, what used to be demonstrated by a desert
is easily made clear by ants.

Now, the ants have stopped their black business,
all lazily gathering around the middle finger of an angel.

You may be wrong about someone, but must admit
you have not been wrong about the world.

Half a month ago, you wanted to invite an ant
into the summer poetry.

So far things have been going so well
that it's like making a movie, the main plot

looks absolutely perfect like a great clue:
you are confronting an ant in the lonely shadow
of an elephant.

1998.7.

Zang Di's poems can be found in *The Book of Cranes: Selected Poems* (Vagabond Press, 2015). Here are additional poems in translation.

绝对的尺度

正午的奇迹仿佛只是
一种垂直的安静。
除了柳叶,天光没有别的脚尖。
水竹的祈祷。以及荷花的手绢
将古老的诱惑重新打包成
一种美好的礼物。
身边,芦苇的尺度大胆到
全是碧绿的缝隙。还有你呢。
全部的心弦也跟着纷纷竖起。

1998.8.

Absolute Scale

The miracle of noon is a vertical tranquility.
Sky light has no toes except the willows.
Water bamboos bend to pray.
Lotus open their palm leaves, the handkerchiefs
to wrap the ancient temptation
into a beautiful gift.
Nearby, reeds are brave, their measurement
full of green splits. And you—you pick up
all your heart and pluck a responding chord.

1998.8.

偶像学

当我靠近时,麻雀飞溅而去,
它们仿佛在表演,
一种我永远也没机会使用的
受惊后的警觉。
在麻雀飞走的地方,
留下来的是蚂蚁——
一队蚂蚁,暧昧于
暂时还没发现别的线索,
列队经过我刚刚投下的阴影。
蚂蚁一点也不惊慌:就好像
我静止在那里,不过是
一个试图思考它们的假象。
更有可能,与飞走的麻雀相比,
我也许只是一根旗杆,
无意中正以抽象的肉为旗帜。

1998.9.

Science of Idols

When I approach, the sparrow splashes away
as if demonstrating an alertness
when startled, something I've never had
a chance to use.
Where the sparrow has flown away
there is a fleet of ants
ambiguously hesitating
as they have found no other clues. Not yet
for the time being. They craw in a line
through the shadow I've just cast.
They are not startled, as if the still body
of mine is but an illusion
or something that's trying to figure them out.
Or even more likely, compared to the flying sparrow
I may just be a flagpole
incidentally taking my abstract flesh as my flag.

1998.9.

作为一个签名的落日丛书

又红又大,它比从前更想做
你在树上的邻居。

凭着这妥协的美,它几乎做到了,
就好像这树枝从宇宙深处伸来。

它把金色翅膀借给了你,
以此表明它不会再对鸟感兴趣。

它只想熔尽它身上的金子,
赶在黑暗伸出大舌头之前。

凭着这最后的浑圆,这意味深长的禁果,
熔掉全部的金子,然后它融入我们身上的黑暗。

2012.11.15.

Sunset as a Signature, A Book Series

Round and red, it wants more than ever
to be your neighbor in the tree.

With a compromising posture, it's almost made it,
as beautiful as ever, branching out from a deep universe.

It has lent its golden wings to you.
It will no longer be interested in birds.

It's burning all the gold in its body
before darkness sticks out its big tongue.

With a final roundedness, a foreseeable forbidden fruit,
it burns and burns into the shadow of your body.

2012.11.15.

莎士比亚的蚂蚁

旁边有枣树，银杏，石榴，
稍远点还有核桃，樱桃，玉兰，
但是，这只蚂蚁却选中
丝瓜的藤蔓，慢慢往上爬。
沿这样的方向，它要寻找的粮食
甚至连你都未必能认出。
也许，它只是刚刚穿过了针眼，
那静止的瓜藤对它来说
不过是一根骆驼毛。
而我突然萌生一种冲动，
渴望管这只蚂蚁叫莎士比亚。

1998.7.

Shakespeare's Ant

Nearby there are ginkgo trees, dates, and pomegranates.
Slightly farther away, walnuts, cherries, and magnolia trees.
But this ant decides
to climb up slowly the vine of sponge gourds.
What kind of food is it looking for in this direction?
Even you may not be able to recognize it.
Perhaps, it has just passed through the eye of a needle.
And the static squash vine is
but a camel's hair in the ant's eye.
And I have a sudden urge
to call it Shakespeare's ant.

1998.7.

腰鼓简史

隐形在空气中,仿佛并不存在,
但高原的阳光,每天都会
提着鞭子,下来检查一遍,
直到它完全成形于看不见的静物;
这里面,究竟有多少依赖
脱俗于生活的惯性,本来就不易觉察;
更难测度的,这无形的依赖中
又会有多少忠诚,直接牵扯到
大地的直觉。此地的风俗包括
你不必焦虑你没时间融入,
你有同样的机会。如果你敲,
你的手,会把你的整个身体
带进一种摸索。开始时,
征兆并不强烈;但很快,
你就会接触到,从未有过
一种人的摸索会如此剧烈。
你抬起的手,从不会落空,
它会落下,像陨石,像下坠的柿子,
将古老的宇宙的分寸,
盲目般击打在我的脸上。
但即使如此,我猜,多数时候
你依然意识不到我的存在。
你认领的,未必是你认出的东西,
而我默认的是,你的,新的摸索
毕竟是从我这里开始的。

2015.1.13.

A Brief History of the Waist Drums

Invisible in the air, as if non-existing,
the sun in the plateau whips it every day
till it's formed into an unnoticeable still life.
Inside it, how much the trust depends on
life's impulse is difficult to detect.
More difficult to measure is how much
this invisible dependence
produces loyalty, directly involving
the intuition of the earth. The customs here:
no need to worry about having no time to be involved,
you'll have the same chance. If you beat (the drum),
your hand will take your entire body
into a kind of exploration. In the beginning
it doesn't feel strong. But soon,
you will encounter a feeling that never before
had a human probing been so powerful.
You lift your hand and it will never reach nothing.
It will drop like a meteorite, a falling persimmon.
An ancient universal appropriateness
strikes my face blindly.
But even so, I guess, most of the time
you don't realize that I exist.
You take what you don't necessarily recognize.
But I take as a default that your new venture
has started from me after all.

2015.1.13.

连翘入门

旁边的迎春花
可不止一簇。你不可将我认错。
你不可偏爱棣棠的企图。
你不可误解我的烂熳
微妙于大地的天真。
如果这是呼吁,那么呐喊已被偏听。
你不可再将我的黄与别的金黄
混淆为人生的疏忽。
最要紧的,你不可将我用一对蝴蝶
击败了世界的主人
解释成:现场已被破坏。

2005

A Guide to the Forsythia Plants

Nearby, there are more than one shrub of spring flowers.
But you shall not be mistaken about me.
You shall not favor the intension of kerria japonica, the flower
Di.
You shall not misunderstand my blooming,
more subtle than the earth's innocence.
If this is a calling, it's been partially heard.
You shall not compare my yellow to the other yellow
and be confused by this as the negligence of life.
Most importantly, when I defeat the world master
with a pair of butterflies, you shall not explain this
as: the scene on the site has been destroyed.

2005

读仓央嘉措丛书

小时候在四川偏僻的集市上
见过的藏族女孩，在你的诗中
已长大成美丽的女人。
你写诗，就好像世界拿她们没办法。
或者，你写诗，就好像时间拿她们没别的办法。
假如你不写诗，你就无法从你身上
辨认出那个最大的雪域之王。
美丽的女人当然是神，
不这么起点，我们怎么会很源泉。
这不同于无论神冒不冒傻气。
她们是她们自己的神，但她们不知道。
或者，她们是她们自己的神
但远不如她们是我们的神。
1987，失恋如同雪崩，我23岁时
你也23岁，区别仅仅在于
我幸存着，而你已被谋杀。
且我们之间还隔着两个百年孤独。
多年来，我接触你的方式
就好像我正沿着你的诗歌时间
悄悄地返回我自己。1989，我25岁时
你22岁，红教的影子比拉萨郊区的湖水还蓝。
1996，我32岁时你19岁，
心声怎么可能只独立于巍巍雪山。
2005，我41岁时你17岁；
一旦反骨和珍珠并列，月亮
便是我们想进入的任何地方的后门。
2014，我50岁时你15岁；
就这样，你的矛盾，剥去年轻的壳后
怎么可能会仅仅是我的秘密。

2014.2.

Reading Tsangyang Gyatso, a Series

The Tibetan girls I saw in my childhood
at a Sichuan Fair, far and remote,
have grown into beautiful women in your poems.
You write as if the world can do nothing about them.
Or, you write as if time can do nothing about them.
If you don't write poetry, you can not recognize in you
the highest king of the snow kingdom.
Beautiful women are gods, of course.
There is no other way to begin than from the beginning.
This is different from whether God is foolish or not.
The women are their own gods but they don't know about it.
Or, they are their own gods—
far less fair than—they are our gods.
1987, I was 23, getting dumped was like an avalanche.
You have been 23, the difference is that
I have survived while you were murdered.
And we are separated by two hundred years of solitude.
Over the years, I approach you in a way
like walking in your poetry
to walk back to myself quietly. 1989, I was 25,
you were 22, the shadow of the red religion was bluer
than the blue water of Lhasa.
1996, I was 32, you were 19,
how can a voice be only independent in snow-capped mountains.
2005, I was 41 and you were 17,
once a rebellious spirit jammed with gems, the moon
became the back door to any place we wanted to enter.
2014, I am 50 and you are 15, as simple as that.
But how can your ambivalence,
stripped off the young shell, be my secret only?
    2014.2

蘑菇丛书

悲观主义者很少会爱上蘑菇,
或像你那样,忠实于蘑菇带给身体的感觉。
常识告诉你,没背叛过虚无的人
不会有兴趣了解蘑菇的精神——
它们的翻滚,甚至比肉体做得还好。

它们翻滚在平底锅里,翻滚在你的喉舌深处。
柔滑,鲜嫩,丝毫也惧怕你
会夺走它们的一切。凡乐观主义者能想到的真理,
它们都会给出一种形状。凡你想隐瞒的事,
它们都能给予最深切的谅解。

它们闻到了小鸡肉的味道。
它们喜爱大蒜和西兰花签下的合同。
它们撑开的伞降落着,降落着,直到在你心里
变成了一个营养丰富的小神。
消失和消化的区别也许

没有你想得那么大。在消失之前,

它们中的一个从里面递出一份新菜谱,
请求下一次你能更耐心地咀嚼
蘑菇身上的暗示。还从未过一种暗示
比它们更接近宇宙的暗示。

2010.11.

Mushroom Series

Pessimists rarely fall in love with mushrooms,
or like you, stay truthful to the physical sensations.
Common sense tells you that unless you betray the Nihilism
you wouldn't be interested in the spirit of mushrooms—
they roll and tumble better than bodies.

They rock n roll in the pan and wheel into your mouth,
tender and fresh, least afraid of being exploited.
Any truth that optimists can think of, they present it
in a shape. Anything you want to conceal,
they perform the profoundest pardon.

They have smelt the taste of little chickens.
They love garlics when they sign a contract with broccolis.
They open their parachutes and fall, till landing in you
and becoming small nutritious gods.
The difference between disappearance and digestion

may not be as big as you thought. Before disappearing,

one of them from inside you will hand out a new recipe
asking you to be more patient next time in tasting
what mushrooms imply. There has never been anything
closer to what the universe implies than mushrooms.

2010.11.

冬天的锤子丛书

空气的锤子落下来
砸在死硬的冻冰上。

我,很像那个被砸过的坑眼,
有人也很像那些飞溅的冰茬;

而锤子使了这么大劲儿,
你应该很像那个听起来很响的声音;

但是很奇怪,我们等了这么久,
却只有喜鹊起伏在美丽的错误中。

2014

Winter Hammer Series

A hammer falls from the air
and hits the dead hard ice.

I am very much like the hole the hammering made.
Some people resemble the splashing of ice.

And after making such a great effort,
the hammer should represent the seemingly loud sound.

But strange enough, we've waited so long,
only magpies fly up and down in the beautiful mistakes.

2014

晚霞丛书

谁制作了它并不重要,
谁能捕捉到它的意义也不重要。
它就像一个巨大的码头,
你能感到有东西靠上去,停了下来,
却说不出那停下的东西是什么。
它把时间变成了时光,
感情的意义因此而不同。
它一出现,就十分清晰,
并一直会将这清晰保持到灿烂。
它从未有过任何模糊的时刻。
它是六月的晚霞,夹在铁灰色的云海之间;
它就像快要被遮没的黑板,
白天的粉笔够不着它,夜晚的粉笔
又总是太迟。它这样向你的记忆迂回,
最有意思的字是曾写下,又被及时擦去的字。
对于那些被擦掉的字,它是一个不会消失的帝国。
它的灿烂很敏感,对称于
人生的缺陷很微妙。你会明白的。
它是时间的风景,但看起来更像是布景。
刚刚结束的白天不完全是一幕戏,
即将开始的夜晚,很难说是不是一出戏。
而它,就像一个准确的角色,
游荡在生活的边缘。它知道你在看它。
它知道你看到它时想说些什么。
但它不知道,你猜不到你是谁,
就仿佛它见过的世面太多了。

2011

Rose Cloud at Sunset

Who has created it doesn't matter.
Who will capture it doesn't matter.
It is there like a huge pier
that you feel something is going up and stops there,
but you can't tell what has stopped there.
It turns time into a scene that how you feel
makes a difference.
It starts as something very clear
and stays clear until it's bright.
It has no blurry moment.
It's the light at sunset in June caught in between
the gray seas of clouds,
like a sinking board about to be obscured,
nothing written on it by the daytime chalks
and too late for the evening crayons.
A detour to remembering. The most interesting words
are those just written but erased on time.
To the erased words, it is an empire
that never disappears. It's brilliant and sensitive,
symmetrical to the subtle regrets
in life. You will understand it in time.
It's the scene of time though it looks like a setup.
The daytime that just ended is not entirely a plot.
It's hard to say if the night that's about to start is a play or not.
It is in itself an accurate character wandering
on the edge of life. It knows you're looking at it.
It knows what you want to say when you see it.
But it doesn't know that it doesn't know who you are
as if it has seen too much.

2011

丹江入门

远远地，我看见它流过
李白的心跳，白居易的肺腑，
杜牧的长恨。多么风貌，
即便是错觉，也自有天意。
头顶上，天是横着的；
以巨石的名义，悬崖叼着好月；
银河更如同放羊的洼地。
想走捷径的话，红泉严格于
缕缕茶香，袅娜你迟早
总会正确于大地上的漫游。
好多后果都很硕大，
比如：仅凭流转的春光，
你就能成就一个人的深爱。
凡妖娆的，必勾连着一个解脱。
放眼望去，越是名花，
越是无主；哪里还轮得着
变形记任性不任性。
忘返的时刻到了。你的感叹
不亚于嘶嘶作响的烙印；
我们送给它一个巨变，
它却从不打算享用。

2015.6.

Entry to the River Ran

In the distance, I see it flow
through Li Bai's heart beating, Bai Juyi's lungs
and Du Mu's eternal grudging. What a scene.
It must be meant to be this way even if an illusion.
Overhead, the sky is horizontally laid out,
cliffs hold a bright moon in the name of boulders,
and the galaxy is more like a sunken prairie for the sheep.
If you want to take a shortcut, you will see ruby springs
follow strict routes, fragrance of tea its own path,
and you will lead your own roaming sooner or later.
Many outcomes are huge consequences.
For example, the wandering around of spring light
can take you deep into someone else's heart.
But anything enchanting will hook up a relief.
Looking around, the more charming some flowers are,
the more ownerless and homeless they are.
The reckless metamorphosis won't help.
It's time to hate to leave. You sigh, and it's no less
than what a hissing iron can do for an impression.
You try to give the river a chance of great change
but it never intends to enjoy it.

2015.6.

试飞协会

在策兰和阿米亥之间,有一个杜甫;
我们应该打一眼井,把他从下面拽上来。
我们总得抽出点时间,听听来自地下的口信。
在阿米亥和特朗斯特吕姆之间,有一个王维;
我们应该把青山挖一个洞,把他从蛇的睡眠王国里唤醒。
在策兰和特朗斯特吕姆之间,有一个李商隐,
我们应该凿开惊呆了的石头,用千年的鸟粪
把他的影子慢慢烤成一块面包。
在阿米亥和泰德休斯之间,有一个姜夔,
我们应该把他从树里抠出来,
放进篮子,再用滑轮和绳子
把他吊到树顶。在那里,
篮子会变回鸟巢。我们仿佛又迂回到了
人和鸟一起试飞的年代。

2014

FLYING ASSOCIATION

Between Celan and Amichai there is a Du Fu.
We should drill a well and draw him up.
Carve out time to listen to the voice from underground.
Between Amichai and Tranströmer, there is a Wang Wei.
We should dig a hole in the green hill to wake him up
from the sleeping realm of snakes.
Between Celan and Tranströmer, there is a Li Shangyin.
We should drill through the stunned stone,
use a thousand year guano to slowly bake his shadow
into a loaf of bread.
Between Amichai and Ted Hughes, there is a Jiang Kui.
We should pull him out of that tree,
put him in a basket, and then, with a pulley and a rope,
haul him up to the treetop. There,
the basket becomes a bird's nest, as if we've wandered
into an age when both men and birds attempt to fly.

2014

纪念维特根斯坦

人死后,鸟继续飞着。
我看着这幕情景。
情景消失后,鸟仍然飞着。
我将关心这样的事情。

维特根斯坦是一只鸟。
以前他不是,但现在是。
以前,人死后,有很多选择,
但很少有人倾向于变成一只鸟。

当然,我也可以这样交代——
以前,我是一只鸟,但现在
我是一个看鸟飞过头顶的人。
飞翔多么纯粹,像冰的自由落体。

我继续这样看下去,
正如维特根斯坦继续巧妙于
一只鸟的名字。空间多么美妙,
就仿佛空间也死过一回。

विट्जेंस्टेंन् की याद में

व्यक्ति की मौत के बाद ,चिड़िया उड़ती रहती है
ये वो दृश्य है जो मै देखता हूँ
जब दृश्य लुप्त होता है ,चिड़िया उड़ना जारी रखती है
मै इस तरह की चीजों की चिंता करता हूँ

विट्जेंस्टेंन् एक चिड़िया है
वह पहले नहीं थी पर अब है
पहले लोगों के पास मरने के बाद बहुत से विकल्प थे
लेकिन थोड़े ही लोग चिड़िया बनने को तैयार होते है

ऐसा क्यों है मै निश्चय ही इसको समझा सकता हूँ
मै पहले चिड़िया था लेकिन अब
मै एक आदमी हूँ जो चिड़ियों को अपने सर के ऊपर उड़ते हुए देखता हूँ
उड़ना उतना निर्मल जितना स्वतंत्र रूप से गिरती हुई बर्फ

मै देखना जारी रखता हूँ
जैसा की विट्जेंस्टेंन् जारी रखता है बद्धिमान होना
चिड़िया के लिए कितनी सूंदर जगह है
उसी तरह जैसे यदि मरने वाले के पास जगह हो

Translated into Hindi by Rahcana Shrivastava

雪说请帮我寻找新的动词丛书

请帮我寻找一个新动词,
它必要于感激的眼睛。白色的动词。
但不必生造:只要在此之前,
它从未被用在我身上就好。
请理解我对新的暗示的无尽的渴求。
请理解我的固执:这个只有你才找得到的动词,
它能帮助记忆复原黑色的战栗。
我的意思是,请看清我是如何行动的——
那么多降落中,只有我专注于最轻盈的暗示。
那么多警惕中,只有我孤独于
安静的死亡。那么多结束中,
只有我新颖于白色的信仰。
请帮我放弃你面对我时习惯用到的动词。
请帮我放弃我的飘,树叶才喜欢飘呢。
请帮我减弱我的飞,帽子才喜欢飞呢。
请帮我亲一下我的融化:我猜想只有你有
种子才会有的秘密而美丽的嘴唇。

Dice la nieve ayúdame a encontrar un verbo nuevo

Ayúdame a encontrar un verbo nuevo—
un verbo que un ojo agradecido anhela. Un verbo blanco.
Pero no inventes uno nuevo: servirá
si antes de hoy nunca se ha utilizado sobre mi cuerpo.
Conoce mi deseo inagotable de hallar una nueva pista.
Conoce mi terquedad: que sólo tú encontrarás aquel verbo,
que ayudará a la memoria a detener su temblor negro.
Quiero decir, ve cómo yo me muevo—
en medio de tanta caída, sólo yo me enfoco en la más ligera clave.
En medio de tanta lucidez, sólo yo siento soledad
en una muerte tranquila. En medio de tanto final,
sólo yo soy nuevo en esta fe blanca.
Ayúdame a renunciar a los verbos que acostumbro cuando me
  enfrentas.
Ayúdame a renunciar a que yo flote, sólo a las hojas les gusta
  flotar.
Ayúdame a debilitar el vuelo, sólo a los sombreros les gusta volar.
Ayúdame a besar lo que se derritió: pienso en que sólo tú tienes labios
tan secretos y tan hermosos como semillas.

Translated into Spanish by Françoise Roy

Poems by Meng Ming 孟明诗选

French translations by Meng Ming except otherwise specified

孟明，1955年出生于海南岛崖县（今三亚市）。年轻时当过知青、码头工人。1987年毕业于中国社会科学院研究生院文史哲部法国语言文学专业。1989年旅居法国至今，长期从事电台记者职业。现居家写作。著有诗集《大记忆书》（安高诗集整理奖，2001年），《槐花之年》（L'Année des fleurs de sophora，汉法双语版，法国Cheyne出版社，2011年），《细色》（华东师范大学出版社，2015年）。译作有《保罗·策兰诗选》（上海，华东师范大学出版社，2010年）；尼采《狄俄尼索斯颂歌》（Dionysos-Dithyramben，上海，华东师范大学出版社，2013年）。曾获奥地利文化部2011年度文学翻译奖。

MENG Ming, born in the South Sea Island of China, graduated from the Academy of Social Sciences in Beijing with an MA in French Literature. He moved to France in 1989 and has worked as a journalist there. His collection of poetry in Chinese won the An Kao Prize in 2001 and his new collection of poetry was published by the East Central China Normal University Press in 2015. His Chinese translation of Collected Poems by Paul Celan was published in China in 2010 winning the translation award in Austria in 2011. His translation of Dionysos-Dithyramben by Nietzsche was published in China in 2013.

未完成的诗

如果她笑,呵,那神气
弥漫于这午夜的沉寂,一场小雨。
我会闻到,大如天神的祭酒闪在门外,
那时,一切都叫做爱情。

一棵冬树。省略。一些事物。
此刻,一支铅笔的暴动
比昨日更悲怆。——这是第几次?
我为你而来,一如人民走向自由。

Un poème inachevé

Si elle rit, ô, de cet air, cet air
qui embrase la nuit silencieuse, il y aura une pluie fine.
Quand venue de l'azur une jarre de deuil descend devant la porte,
je sais, tout sera nommé Amour.

Un arbre hivernal. Une éclipse. Et certaines choses.
Mais ici, soulèvement d'un crayon,
plus violent qu'hier. – Pour combien de fois déjà ?
je viens à toi, comme un peuple s'achemine vers la liberté.

去玳瑁岛

那年夏天，说去玳瑁岛，
我们从沙丘跑下来，拖着
早已朽烂的天使船，碎木横飞，
像树上落下鸟巢。起风了，
你在夕阳里，我在浪花里。

我不知道，天地
作合真有前世和未来？
指派给人的，想必有其道理，
譬如落水死去，或者远行他乡。

记得，站在沙丘顶上，
我们望见——
那岛驮着青山，波涛滚滚。
那是很久以前的事了，
仿佛今生再无来世。

词语太轻，姐姐，
还用浮木，为我奏飓风歌。

击弦风来，如坐舟中。
那是甚么韵律，你为我
解衣作帆。你手巧，
长锁短锁，勾剔吟猱，
一夜舟，七年路。你说那曲调无文字，
何又熟若一支旧谱？
姐姐，玳瑁岛从未存在。

Vers l'île Daimao

Pour aller, cet été, sur l'île Daimao,
nous descendîmes la dune en traînant
notre bateau angélique, qui pourri s'éparpilla
comme un nid d'oiseau tombé d'un arbre. Le vent se lève.
Te voilà dans le soleil couchant. Moi, dans les flots.

Je ne sais pas, comme promis par le ciel et la terre,
si l'anneau reliera la vie antérieure à l'avenir.
Ce qui est destiné doit avoir une raison,
noyade, ou bien voyage vers le lointain ?

Mais debout sur la dune, je m'en souviens,
nous voyions au loin…
L'île portait ses collines vertes parmi les vagues.
Cela doit être ainsi depuis longtemps,
comme si la vie d'ici était sans karma.

Les mots sont trop légers, Sœur, prends plutôt
les bois flottants et joue-moi un chant de tempête.

Vint le vent dans les cordes, comme si l'on était dans une barque,
mais d'où venait ce rythme ? Tu enlevas tes habits
pour m'en faire une voile, et tes doigts, si habiles,
enchaînèrent mille sons tantôt longs et tantôt brefs.
Une nuit en mer, sept ans de route. Cette musique, dis-tu,
est sans tablature, pourquoi est-elle si familière ?
Sœur, l'île Daimao n'a jamais existé.

汉俳四题

1

雨水剪寒枝,
三下两下
打发了那古老的死无常。

2

一只手在萤火里招呼。
山风过路,夏草蛇行:你的歌。

3

今年,看山,
千红不慰一叶血,心中
最后一片叶也落地了。

4

把酒坐进冬天,
吟么吟,山青青,
似曾相识的影子过山来。

Haïku à quatre thèmes

1

la pluie taille les rameaux hivernaux,
d'un coup, trois coups,
elle chasse le vieil Inconstant.

2
une main fait signe dans les lucioles,
et voilà que dans le vent qui passe
les herbes d'été dansent
avec le serpent : c'est ton chant.

3
en regardant la montagne,
le foisonnement du rouge, inconsolable,
la dernière foliole tombe sur la terre.

4
un verre à la main assis dans l'hiver,
rime sur rime, verdure sur verdure,
les ombres déjà vues reviennent par les crêtes.

外婆的驱魔术

门上，一盏葫芦灯
照亮时间以内，以外；
石灰，已撒在房屋四周。
竹枝嘭嘭打出几个头脸来，
蜥易血滴入黄米酒。

你喝了。顺着你的血管
那蜥易拖着透明的鳞甲爬回山中。
你想它慢吞吞的样子，
会不会死在路上。

外婆说
鬼的世界比人的大。你急于
看见那东西，它的模样
也许就是一只死蜥易的灵魂。

一夜之死，
四月之棺透明。
所有的问题都在来去中，
理解，月相已朝西。

蜥易驮着你的病走了。
哪里又有终结？
不懂家山，就不懂天命。那次死亡
不是比今生更让人感动？

La grand-mère magique

Devant la porte une lampe en calebasse
éclaire le temps en deça et au-delà; la chaux
autour de la maison est répandue. Au boum-boum
du bambou surgissent des têtes cornues,
le sang d'un lézard tombe dans l'alcool jaune.

Tu l'as bu. Alors le lézard dans tes veines
traînant sa cuirasse transparente retourne
dans la montagne. Il marche si lentement
que tu as peur qu'il ne meurt en chemin.

Grand-mère disait
l'univers des diables est plus grand que celui des hommes.
Tu t'efforces de discerner cette chose qui est là,
ce n'est qu'une forme qui ressemble à l'âme d'un lézard mort.

Mort d'une nuit,
cadavre cristallin d'avril.
Tous les problèmes sont dans ce qui va et qui revient,
il n'est que la phase lunaire tournée vers l'ouest.

Le lézard est reparti en emportant ta maladie.
Où est donc la fin de la fin ? Qui ignore
La montagne ne comprendra pas le destin. Cette mort-là
n'est-elle pas plus émouvante que la vie d'ici ?

神意裁判

失去中心，老宅里藏匿的石人
全都逃到门外，——不是心灵，
绝不是。如地上砰然心跳的瓦罐倾倒出
苡米和叹息；或者，一只船被风
击碎了，人在岸上哭海。而生活始终平静，
如荒人在暮色里听狗叫。

这些人，隐秘家族，怎样来
又怎样制造他们的出场者？瞬间
竹烟筒扔了一地。海市如沙，
黏在皮肤有坐入大地的快感。
呼唤，来自低矮的房子，
常年飘着咸鱼和海水气味的街道。

走出去就能看见，水重复
每日的集市，也重复着挑担过桥的
七姊妹。哦，那些皮肤晒黑的
女人（她们或许就是一个）。
命运的判别已成了一部世说新语，
七这个没有意义的虚数也变得重要。

这地方，七可能意味着十个葬礼
或者四十九只天鹅从未亡人的宅顶飞过。
天空依旧，农事依旧，街上卖肉，
邻人授衣备食。虚数使我们不安，
或以它古老的数相使人丁兴旺，
或以其溢美的习俗杀死一个不慎的诗人。

Ordalie

Ayant perdu le centre, les têtes de pierre enfouies ont toutes
déserté leur site ancien — ce ne sont pas les âmes, certes non,
qui se répandent le cœur battant, comme d'une jarre renversée
tels soupirs et larmes-de-Job. Ou plutôt, devant un bateau
fracassé par le vent,
les gens sur la rive pleurant les disparus. La vie reste pourtant tranquille,
ainsi le crépuscule, une ombre à canne suit son chemin aux aboiements.

Comment sont-ils venus ces hommes, ce clan secret,
et comment s'est montée leur entrée en scène ? En un clin d'œil
les pipes de bambou jonchèrent le sol. Mirages comme de sable,
ivresse collant à la peau, je me sens perdu pour m'ancrer dans la terre.
Un appel, qui venait des maisons basses, et cette rue
où règne à longueur d'année l'odeur de la mer et du poisson salé.

Dès qu'on sort apparaît le marché qui chaque jour renaît des eaux,
et aussi, marchant sans trêve de ce côté du pont vers l'autre rive
sept filles. Oui ce sont, pareillement brunies par le soleil
sept filles toutes semblables (à moins qu'elles ne soient qu'une).
Or les arrêts de nos destins sont devenus nouveaux Propos mondains,
Et sept, ce nombre imaginaire sans signification, a pris de
l'importance.

Ici, sept peut signifier dix enterrements, ou alors
quarante neuf cygnes survolant la maison des veuves
sous le ciel inchangé, la terre à travailler, la viande à débiter,
le voisinage se procure habits et nourriture. Mais ce nombre nous inquiète,
ou de sa figure antique il fait prospérer les familles,
ou de ses mœurs flagorneuses il tue un poète insouciant.

Traduit du chinois par Emmanuelle Péchenart

时间和两个人

对面,是什么?是沙堆和缺口,
是桌子的长度和一个女人用肘臂托起
沉寂,像母亲托起孩子的头
放进时间对面的海。

记得她,也就记得沙地,石灰窑,
从大木桶拖出树皮浸染的船,
载着一只捕获的红鹿。不要回头,你会
使我成为命运这个词并为之静静地拥有。

真的。一张瘦削的脸,闪过木桩,
在玻璃窗上显出海的流逝,我没有
听见那些伤害从铺满针叶的海上走来。
是啊,那女人把你带到雨落下的地方

也就结束了。结束了,她说。
你们在这双重的故事里离开家,
船坏了,石灰窑也废弃了,
父亲死了,没有人再出海去採石灰石。

后来,关于那件事(我们在林中
的事)你说最好把它放回黎人古老的传说,
以后我们还可以回到它的木麻黄林,
重新讲述一只红鹿的故事。

对面是 S 地,生活着的人;经过沙丘
的缺口。她来。她坐下,开始讲述,
我们都在平常的日子里讲述,像陌生人
谈论家乡、石灰、红鹿、父亲的死

以及那失语的时代最美的记忆。
它消除了我的时间,而我总在追问对面,
是否来临如同逝去?对面,是一个女人
在沉默中为我托起生活高贵的头。

    1998 年 6 月

Deux personnes et le temps

Qu'est-ce qu'il y a en face ? Il y a les tas de sables et les brèches,
il y a la longueur de la table avec une femme qui soutient de son coude
le silence, comme une mère soutient la tête de son enfant
pour le déposer face au temps dans la mer.

Se souvenir d'elle, c'est se souvenir de l'étendue de sable, des fours à chaux,
sortir d'un grand tonneau de bois un bateau teint d'écorces brunes,
qui transporte un cerf rouge capturé. Ne te retourne pas, tu pourrais
faire de moi ce mot, destin, et en devenir le territoire.

Vraiment. Un visage creusé passe en un éclair le pieu d'amarrage
et paraît sur les carreaux l'image du ressac. Je n'ai pas
entendu ces blessures monter de la mer couverte d'aiguilles de pin.
Oui, cette fille t'a conduit là où la pluie tombe

Et c'est terminé. Fini, dit-elle. Vous deux
dans ce double récit vous êtes séparés et partis loin de la maison.
Le bateau est hors d'usage, le four à chaux désaffecté
depuis la mort du père personne ne va plus en mer chercher la craie.

Par la suite, à propos de cette histoire (ce qui nous est arrivé
dans la forêt) tu dis laissons-la donc rejoindre les vieilles légendes des Li,
plus tard nous pourrons retourner dans son bois de filaos
pour raconter encore, toujours à propos d'un cerf rouge.

En face, il y a le village, et des gens qui vivent ; c'est au-delà de la brèche
dans les dunes. Elle vient. Elle s'assied, commence à raconter,
tous les jours ordinaires nous racontons, comme des inconnus
qui discutent du pays, de la chaux, des cerfs rouges et de la mort d'un père

Et aussi des plus beaux souvenirs de cet âge aphasique.
Ils ont éliminé le temps, et me voilà qui toujours cherche à savoir, en face,
n'est-ce pas aussi bien passé qu'à venir ? En face, il y a une femme
qui pour moi, en silence, soutient de son bras la tête précieuse de
l'existence.

       Traduit du chinois par Emmanuelle Péchenart

花开着。没有土地

花开着。没有土地,母亲
不是土地。只有台阶上的人,
弯腰,用木盆晒水,在石上捣苦艾草。
大风吹过,你坐在盐田
心事如盐。关于大地你能说什么?

能否找到相似的事物?
你踏着大地的幻想
　　　在词语中流亡。
你举出例子,那秋天的诗人
在格罗岱克,夜里风车木翼断了。
没有大地,木翼断了,妹妹穿着白衣
来到你和混战流血的伙伴中间,而你
拿起书本,血泊已浸透书页
——你唯一的大地。
她来,手放在你脸上,云轻轻飘过
如果这是你的大地,开着花,白色的凤仙花
白是你早年的幻觉经验,坚实的
靠得住,你就不会失去。

在烫脚的石上,母亲
捣油枯,她年年晒水洗头,
用苦艾擦身,擦血和伤
这就是你寻找大地的理由吧——

那里生长着多根的人
血红色的旧河岸,妹妹的鞋
在红土路的光芒里发出噗噗的响声
那急促地踢着地上落叶的怪癖。

Florifère. Loin du sol

Florifère. Loin du sol, une mère
ce n'est pas un sol. Seule, la personne sur les marches,
écrase de l'absinthe sur la pierre, fait tiédir l'eau au soleil.
Passe une bourrasque, assis dans les marais salants
tu roules des pensées comme du sel. Que dire, à propos de cette terre ?

Peut-on imaginer quelque chose de comparable ?
Tu foules cette terre, ses illusions,
                      et tu t'exiles dans les mots
comme si tu pouvais faire des parallèles : un poète de l'automne
à Grodek, la nuit, une aile de l'éolienne s'est rompue.
Loin de la terre, l'aile de bois est cassée. Sœur, vêtue de blanc,
arrive parmi vous, toi et tes camarades qui saignez de vous être battus, et
quand tu reprends ton livre, le sang en a trempé les feuilles
— la terre, la seule qui te reste.
Elle vient, pose ses mains sur ton visage, où se dispersent les nuages.
Si la voilà, ta terre, avec ses fleurs, des balsamines blanches,
si le blanc est l'expérience hallucinée de tes jeunes années, solide
et sûr, alors tu ne la perdras pas.

Sur la pierre brûlante, mère
écrase le tourteau, chauffe l'eau au soleil, une saison suivant l'autre,
se lave la tête, frotte son corps à l'absinthe, frotte le sang et les blessures.
Est-ce pour cela que tu la cherches, la terre —

Là où croissent des gens aux nombreuses racines,
la vieille rive rouge sang, et sœur dont les chaussures
sonnent dans l'éclat aveuglant du chemin de terre rouge
avec sa manie de faire voler à coups de pied les feuilles mortes.

        Traduit du chinois par Emmanuelle Péchenart

石灰走道

潜入预感的那些力量,
来自家神和土地的一个古老意念。
那声音,是否比命运更沉重?

你要回去,回到一座岛,
伊人领你走进盐田,
走到你曾爬过的木风车底下。

母亲倚门。风从沙丘吹来
吹来你戴上草帽就走了,跟着旧人;
山根纸钱飘灰时,你站在

斑蚀的墓前。某个冬日,
灰濛濛的,你扯着他的大衣角,
小跑着经过那条唯一的石灰走道。

镇子。海的声音就在不远处,
你已经成年。那种在飞沫上破碎的东西
还能听见。说话吧,父亲,

我在你的声音里躲藏,就像小时候
我躲在你的大衣底下……

    1992 年 9 月 24 日

Chemin de craie

Une force se cache sous le pressentiment,
elle est venue de nos terres et de nos dieux familiers.
Sa voix n'a-t-elle pas plus de poids que le destin ?

Tu as voulu repartir, retrouver une île
où l'amante d'hier t'avait conduit dans les marais salants
sous l'éolienne dont tu escaladais jadis les montants de bois.

Mère s'appuie sur la porte. Le vent souffle des dunes
Et tu t'envoles avec ton chapeau de paille à la poursuite de
l'amante.
Les liasses de monnaie funéraire une fois consumées, tu te tiens

debout sur une tombe en ruine. En quelque jour d'hiver
si sombre, agrippé au pan de son manteau
tu avais couru jusqu'au bout du seul chemin de craie.

Le bourg. Le bruit de la mer est tout proche,
tu as maintenant atteint l'âge adulte. Tu entends encore ceci
qui se brisait dans les embruns. Parle-moi, père –

Je me cacherai dans ta voix, comme je l'ai fait
tout petit, dans les plis de ton manteau…

      Traduit du chinois par Emmanuelle Péchenart

槐花之年

    给 H. Y.

女人啊，我们望见外面那红月亮，
匍伏于山岗像苍老的袄教徒的记忆，
守夜者又在下面摇起火把了。

人鬼张望着走进窄门之夜，
你来了像个疯女人砸了房子的木板，
又见槐花，静得像是一场花葬。

安睡。——湖泊之光
我梦见巫女夜夜歌唱。有一次
去旅行，听见那夜歌引诱我

爬了七层楼。像亡命者寻找
一个湖泊，那可追寻的和不可追寻的，
索性亡命天涯，毁掉手稿。

你的方言里有蒲草，船和山城，
夜是可渡的，夜使人湮没。至少
我们可以像故事里的人把船推到对岸。

太荒唐了。你的嘴角挂着狡黠，
总是把我捆在你的湖面用你的方言
说话。要知道，这城市已宣布戒严，

我们将度过这个夏天，
这个像湖岛飘满槐花的夏天，
然后干涸。然后你乘火车去南方。

        1990 年 2 月 29 日

L'année des fleurs de sophora
Pour H. Y.

Ô femmes, nous regardons au dehors la lune rouge,
elle rampe sur les hauteurs comme le souvenir d'un vieux zoroastrien,
le veilleur en bas a recommencé d'agiter sa torche.

Par des lacunes du jour fantômes et humains alarmés entrent dans la nuit,
toi tu es venue comme une folle et tu fais voler en éclats les planches,
voilà revenues les fleurs du sophora. Aussi tranquille qu'un
catafalque fleuri

sommeil paisible. — Lumières sur le lac
en rêve j'entendais chaque nuit chanter les sorcières. Une fois
j'étais en voyage, leur chant nocturne m'a envoûté,

j'ai grimpé les sept étages. Comme un banni recherche
une rive, celle qu'on peut et qu'on ne peut pas poursuivre,
il a fallu partir loin, détruire les manuscrits.

Dans ton dialecte il y a l'acore odorant, l'embarcation, le bourg de montagne
et la nuit que nous traversons, en elle sombrait l'humanité. Au moins
pouvons-nous comme ces personnages du conte conduire le
bateau à bon port.

C'est si absurde. Toi, la malice au coin des lèvres
tu me retiens attaché à ton lac, en me parlant
dans ta langue. Il fallait le savoir : cette ville était sous la loi martiale.

Nous devrons passer l'été ici,
cet été comme une île où pleuvent les fleurs de sophora.
Mais tout flétrira, tu prendras le train vers le Sud.

Traduit du chinois par Emmanuelle Péchenart

关于新诗危机的一次对话

臧棣

B：你为什么不承认当代诗有危机？
Z：因为对当代诗来说，我们还处于巨大的诗歌机遇之中。我们还远远没有穷尽新诗的可能性。所谓当代诗的危机，在我看来，一半是庸人自扰，一半是杞人忧天。

中国新诗的问题，从根本上说，并非是一个是继承还是反叛传统的问题。而是由于现代性的介入、世界历史的整体化发展趋向、多元文化的渗透、社会结构的大变动（包括旧制度的解体和新体制的建立），在传统之外出现了一个越来越开阔的新的审美空间。
中国古典诗歌仍是一个不容忽视的文学资源。
旧诗对新诗的影响，以及新诗借鉴于旧诗其间所体现出的文学关联不是一种继承关系，而是一种重新解释的关系。

从写作的角度看诗的技艺，我们或许会意识到，技巧问题在本质上是一个责任问题。
换句话说，在诗歌中，讲究技巧会促使诗人尽力忠实于诗的责任。
诗的技巧，某种意义上，也是一份语言的契约。
好的诗造就了在我们的生命意识中一种语言的氛围。
身为诗人，我们想像组织语言那样组织形式。但最终我们发现，我们只能组织语言，无法组织形式。开放的形式也好，封闭的形式也好，就风格意识而言，其实只和艺术的功效有关，其次牵扯到一点写作的快感。所以，到后来我们还是要面对形式的核心问题：形式的责任。形式的责任不过是令经验感到深刻的惊异。
没有挑战过形式的诗人，或许可以把诗侍弄得还那么回事，但他们不会领悟到诗的愉悦意味着什么。

面具，是诗歌送给语言的最好的礼物，但却引发了巨大的误解。很多人甚至完全弄拧了，在它们看来，面具本该是语言送给诗歌的最好的礼物。

诗人的直觉从本质上讲是一种文化能力。它与个人的天赋有关，也能激发个人的才能，但它具有强烈的非个人特征，它寓于文化共同体之中，召唤的是最根本的文化洞察力。

与其说新诗发现并诊断了一种汉语的疾病，莫如说新诗发明并拓展了一种语言的治疗。

一天之内，你读过或识别过的好诗最好不要超过五首。这迷信 听起来古怪却未必是无的放矢。

阅读好诗绝对是一种体力活。

只有好诗才谈得上有耐心。好诗的耐心就像一座深山。你出发的时候，什么是宝藏似乎很明确。一旦你抵达那里，身在其中，什么是宝藏就有点微妙了。

就创造与写作的关联而言，新诗也可以说是非常幸运的。在新诗的诞生中一直伴随有两种强烈的召唤：来自形式的召唤，来自语言的召唤。

散文已成为诗的秘密。就独创性而言，这的确是最令我们吃惊的语言情形。

人们喜欢谈论海子的天才，却很少能惊觉到，海子真正了不起的地方就是，他在自杀之前已亲手谋杀了一个天才的海子。

某种程度上，也可以这样讲，海子的天才就在于他一直激烈地拒绝完成一个真正的海子。

最新发现的诗歌元素：佩索阿身上有一个贝克特。

A：你的诗歌具有一种侵略性。
Z：诗对平庸确实有强烈的侵略性。伟大的诗更是如此。

也可以这样谈论诗的精确，我们可以精确到将想象力作为一种诗的器官。

伟大的诗对循环怀有一种独特的兴趣。也不妨说，面对时事和世事的纷杂，伟大的诗创造出了一种对时间的循环的独特的信任。

诗的循环让心灵和语言成为彼此的镜像。

诗的高贵暧昧于诗的多样性。

在最好的诗的语言中，从来就没有孤独。这或许也是汉语诗歌带给世界文学的一种最独特的遗产。

杜甫的伟大绕不过陶渊明，但陶潜的伟大却可以绕过杜甫。

在诗人的背后，始终是一个充满陷阱的话题。诸如，在海子的背后有一个洛尔迦。在穆旦的背后有一个到过武汉的奥登。在奥登的背后有一个自新的拜伦。在卞之琳的背后有一个爱睡懒觉的莎士比亚。但是，很奇怪，在莎士比亚的背后却没有任何人。其实，在诗人的背后，除了我们自己，本不该有其他的人出没。

我不是在反思什么，也不是在暗示什么，我只是说，在某种意义上，作为用现代汉语写诗的人，我们都是卞之琳。这样说的目的，不是说我们都要成为卞之琳那样的诗人。而是说，只要用现代汉语写，不论我们的写作起点从哪里开始，我们都会路过卞之琳。

你可以这样看，顾城是卞之琳发明出来的语感的一种延伸。也可以这样说，卞之琳不过是顾城的另一个版本。他们两人之间的关联，就像诗歌史里存在着暗道一样。

中国的古诗，其实很现代，也很后现代。但如果拘泥于我们对传统抱有的那种传统主义的臆想，我们当然无法看出古诗是怎么现代的，更无法窥探到古诗是如何后现代的。

对诗人而言，汉语是否是世界上最适合写诗的语言，并不重要。重要的是，汉语有没有足够的语言弹性。幸运的是，由于有了现代汉语的诗歌实践，汉语变得更富有弹性了。

在新诗与古诗的争执中，新诗最核心的思想命题是，我们必须学会医治汉语。古代汉语无涉语言的自我治疗，这必然会在语言的历史向度上导致活力的丧失，并造成想象力的贫乏和虚弱。而新诗的呼吁，其实也很简单：是到了该医治汉语的时候了。

从诗学的战术的角度看，超越传统，反传统，回归传统，都可能是一副好牌。但当代诗学不能仅仅满足于打出好牌，还应确立一种更深邃的战略目标。对当代诗学来说，最迫切的任务是，重新建构当代诗与传统的关联。这种新的关联，意味着我们不再将诗的可能性归结于反对传统，或是回归传统，抑或超越传统。

大诗人的工作不是弥合矛盾，而是加深矛盾。大诗人用一种奇异的平衡加深着人们所说的矛盾。对诗歌而言，随着矛盾的加深，反而会出现了新的可能性。

最令西方诗学不解的是，我们的古典传统缺少对"伟大"这一维度的文学认知，但却写出足够伟大的作品。但我的问题是，那可能意味着古典写作的特殊的幸运，并不意味着我们的当代写作能幸运地继承这种幸运。

迄今为止，我们的诗歌史写作犯下的一个最明显的错误是，我们没能意识到，除了是名词之外，传统也是一个"动词"。我们的诗歌史写作应该学会将传统作为一个动词来使用。

这或许是新诗上最值得玩味的时刻：在新诗开始它的语言实践之初，新诗是传统的一个例子，尽管传统并不打算正式面对它。而随着新诗的实践接近百岁，传统反倒变成了新诗的一个例子。这种反转，对诗歌史的写作来说，是一个难得的机遇。

朦胧诗只是为一种诗歌史写作的诗。这不是朦胧诗的错，也不是诗歌史的错，这只是一种可以借鉴的错误。

诗没有危机感。这是诗的高贵的一个具体的表现。也许某些诗人会在特定的文化语境里感到某些危机，但那只是他个人要解决的事情。

危机感只是人们对诗做出的一种廉价的反应。之所以廉价，就在于这种反应是建立在诗的功利基础上的。

（截选）

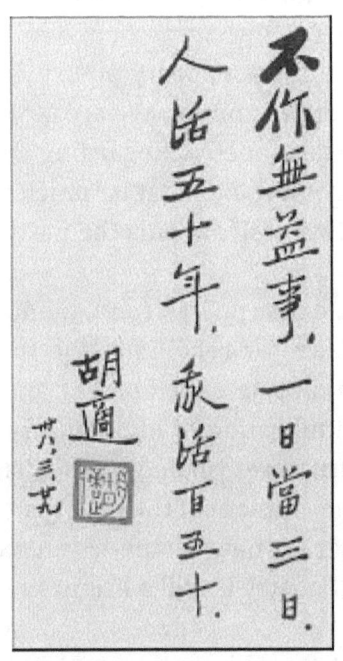

Calligraphy by Hu Shi, founder of New Poetry in China

IS THERE A CRISIS IN CHINESE NEW POETRY?

Zang Di

B: Why don't you acknowledge that there is a crisis in contemporary Chinese poetry?

Z: Because as far as contemporary poetry is concerned, we are facing tremendous opportunities. We are far from exhausting the possibilities of the new poetry. Regarding the crisis of contemporary poetry, in my view, half of it is "much ado about nothing", the other half "the fear of ill exceeds the ills we fear."

The issue for Chinese new poetry, fundamentally speaking, is not an issue of inheritance or rebellion. Due to the intervening of modernity, the trend of its development and integration in the world history, the infiltration of multiculturalism, and the great changes of social structures (including the dismantling of the old system and the establishment of the new system), there is a more and more open space for new aesthetics outside the tradition.

Chinese classical poetry is still a literary resource that cannot be ignored.

The influence of the old poetry on the new poetry and the relationship between the two as a result of using the old poetry as a reference for the new poetry is not a relationship of inheritance, but of reinterpretation of the old by the new.

From the perspective of the craftsman of poetry writing, we may realize that the issue of craftsmanship is essentially a responsibility.

In other words, to pay attention to the crafts it will encourage the poets to be faithful to the responsibility of poetry.

Poetry craftsmanship, in a sense, is also a contract with language.

A good poem creates a linguistic atmosphere in our consciousness of life.

As poets, we imagine establishing a form in the same way as establishing a language. But in the end we realize that we can only establishing a language. Whether opened or closed, form only relates to the effectiveness of art, followed by a pleasure of writing. Therefore, in the end we still have to face the core issue of form: responsibility of form. The responsibility of form is nothing but a profound surprise to our experience.

Those who have not challenged the form may be able to make a poem so much as to pass the standard but they will not know what the pleasure of poetry is.

Mask is the best gift of poetry to the language, but it has triggered a huge misunderstanding. Many people have even completely screwed it up in thinking that mask should be the best gift of language to poetry.

The intuition of a poet is, in essence, a cultural ability. It is related to individual talent as well as to stimulate individual talent, but it has a strong non-personal characteristics which resides in the cultural community, a call for the most fundamental cultural insight.

Rather than discovering and diagnosing a disease of Chinese language, the new poetry has invented a treatment of language.

Within one day, it is better that you read or identify no more than five good poems. This superstition sounds strange but may not be pointless.

Reading a good poem is definitely a manual labor.

Only a good poem can be relevant to patience. The patience of a good poem is like a deep mountain. When you start off, what is a treasure seems to be very clear. Once you get there and you are inside it, what is a treasure becomes a delicate issue.

As for the connection between creativity and writing, the new poetry can be said to be very lucky. From its birth, the new poetry has been accompanied by two strong calls: from form and language.

Prose has become the secret of poetry. In terms of originality, this is indeed the most surprising linguistic situation.

People like to talk about Hai Zi as a genius, but few have been alert to this finding: what's most amazing about Hai Zi is that he had personally killed the genius in him before he committed suicide.

To some extent, it can be said that Hai Zi was a genius in that he fiercely refused to become a real Hai Zi.

The newly discovered poetics: Pessoa has a Beckett behind him.

A: Your poetry has an invasive element.
Z: Poetry should indeed be strongly invasive against mediocrity. Great poetry should be even more so.

It is also possible to talk about the accuracy of poetry this way. We can be so precise as to taking imagination as a body organ of poetry.

Great poetry has a unique interest in the cycle. We might as well say that in facing the complex of current situation, great poetry has created a unique trust in the circle of time.

The cycle of poetry makes the mind and language mirroring each other.

Poetic elegance is ambiguous in that poetry is diversified.

In the supreme language of poetry there is no solitude. This is perhaps the most unique heritage of Chinese poetry to the world literature.

Du Fu's greatness cannot be talked about without mentioning Tao Yuanming. But not vise versa.

Behind poets there is always a topic full of traps. For example, there is a Lorca behind Hai Zi. Behind Mu Dan there is an Auden who's been to Wuhan. Behind Auden there is a revived Byron. Behind Bian Zhilin is Shakespeare who loved to get up late.

However, it is strange that there is no one behind Shakespeare. In fact, there should be no one else coming and going behind us but ourselves.

I am not trying to imply anything. I am just saying that, in a sense, as modern Chinese poets, we are all Bian Zhilin. By saying so I don't mean we have to become Bian Zhilin, but that, as long as we use modern Chinese to write poetry, regardless of where the starting point of our writing may be, we will pass Bian Zhilin.

You can see Gu Cheng as the extension of what Bian Zhilin invented as a sense of language. It can also be said that Bian Zhilin was another version of Gu Cheng. The relationship between the two of them indicates that there are hidden channels in the history of poetry.

The ancient Chinese poetry is, in fact, very modern and also very post-modern. However, if we cling to our traditional imagination of the tradition, we certainly cannot see how it's modern, nor how it's post-modern.

Whether Chinese is the world's most suitable language for writing poetry or not is not important. What's important is whether Chinese has sufficient linguistic resilience. Fortunately, thanks to the practice of modern Chinese poetry, Chinese has become more resilient.

In the dispute between new poetry and ancient poetry, the core of the new poetry proposition is that we must learn to heal Chinese. Ancient Chinese was not concerned about language self-treatment. It inevitably leads to the loss of vitality in terms of historical dimensions of language and leads to the impoverishment of imagination. The call of new poetry is, in fact, very simple: it is time to cure Chinese.

From the perspective of poetic tactics, to bypass the tradition, to act against the tradition or to return to the tradition is likely a good card in each to play. However, contemporary poetics cannot just be satisfied with playing good cards. We should establish more profound strategic objectives. For contemporary poetics, the most urgent task is to reconstruct the connection between contemporary poetry and tradition. This new connection means that we no longer attribute the possibility of poetry to the opposition to tradition, a return to tradition, or a bypass of tradition.

The work of the great poets is not to minimize conflicts, but to sharpen the conflicts. The great poets deepen what people call as conflicts or contradictions by using a strange balance. For poetry, with the sharpening/deepening of conflicts, new possibility will come along.

What is most puzzling to Western poetics is that our classical tradition lacks literary awareness of the dimension of "greatness", but has produced great works. But my concern is, it may mean the classical writing has a special luck but does not mean our contemporary writing can lucky inherit that luckiness.

One of the most obvious mistakes we have made so far in our history of poetry writing is that we fail to realize that tradition is a "verb" in addition to being a noun. Our history of poetry writing should learn to use tradition as a verb.

This is perhaps the most interesting moment in new poetry: at the beginning of its language practice, poetry is an example of tradition, although tradition does not intend to face it formally. And with the practice of new poetry for a hundred years, tradition has become an example of the new poetry. This reversal, as far as history of poetry is concerned, is a rare opportunity.

Misty poetry was written for history. This is not misty poetry's fault, nor history's fault. This is just a mistake poetry can learn from.

Poetry has no sense of crisis, which is a manifestation of the noble state of poetry. Perhaps some poets feel certain crises in a particular cultural context, but that's only his personal problem to be resolved personally.

A sense of crisis is just an inexpensive response to poetry. It is cheap in that it is a reaction based on the utilitarian belief of poetry.　　(Excerpt)

一篇被法镭搅了局的诗论

杨小滨

我最近常常被那个叫做法镭的家伙搞得六神无主。比如，当我现在要下笔写一篇严肃的诗论时，法镭发了一条微信给我，说这篇文章应当这样开头：我看见这一代精英被各种辉煌的理念毁灭成正义的幻影……

这到底是什么意思？其实，我一直以这个时代的精英兄弟们而自豪。我本来想写的是另外一句话：在这个主流话语仍然以宏大的虚假希望主导着我们语言体系的时代，越来越多的诗人从空洞洪亮的合唱队中毅然撤离，发出自己异质的声音，这无疑是中国当代诗歌的希望所在。

我听见了法镭在远处的窃笑声。呃，好吧。的确，从百年前新诗的开端，经过了朦胧诗、后朦胧诗的喧闹，一直到今天依旧强劲的诗歌主潮，诗人们对自我的确信也建立起了另一种神话：主体的神话。那些自我中心的抒情主体占据了诗歌写作的核心，仿佛主体的声音是全然自足的，绝对可信的。法镭，这是你想说的吧？那我就顺着你的思路继续。

这个主体从整一化自我的声音出发，致力于表达情感和观念，无论是郭沫若式的天狗，徐志摩式的雪花，还是郭路生式的知青，王家新式的受难者；无论是朝向大海和天空，还是面对历史和社会。这在五四时代和后文革时代似乎都是不言自明的：文学必须从伦常社会或集体狂热中解放出来，回到自我的"真诚"表达。但事实是，抒情的"小我"总是不自觉地靠向作为他者的"大我"，并且依赖于"大我"的宏大理念：因为唯有"大我"才能保证"小我"的合法性。在我们当今的文学话语里，从来不缺"大我"的旗帜。当然，"大我"总是代表了正义，谁又敢说半个不字呢？

法镭从手机里探出头来打断我：其实，徐志摩还写过《变与不变》这样——用你们理论家常喜欢引用的巴赫金的行话来说——"众声喧哗"的诗。诗中除了树叶和星星，抒情主体甚至分裂成"答话"的"心"和"插话"的"灵魂"。就像你和我，他补充说。

　　我吃了一惊，法镭知道的太多了。静下来一想，我更感兴趣的，却是鲁迅的那首《我的失恋》。虽说自称为打油诗，却一举消灭了所有以自我为中心的新诗。是吗，法镭问道，为什么？我想了想，应该是因为诗中的"我"和鲁迅没有半点关系，鲁迅创造了一个面具化的荒诞主体，从而消解了那个可能会表达伟大爱情观念的现代主体。鲁迅可能是二十世纪中国文学最早的后现代主义者。写到这里，恰好看到张枣的一句话："作为新诗现代性的写作者，胡适毫无意义，也无需被重写的文学史提及。我们新诗之父是鲁迅，新诗的现代性其实有着深远的鲁迅精神……"。我想也许可以把"现代性"看作是"后现代性"，反正利奥塔认为现代必须首先是后现代的。在《狗的驳诘》里，鲁迅塑造了一个连狗都辩驳不了的贫乏主体。在《野草》的许多篇章里，鲁迅也应和了超现实主义对梦境的迷恋。

　　那么，也可以说，我的每一首诗都是梦境的。因为梦里超现实的我不必是现实的我。梦里的我不过是法镭罢了。刚说罢，法镭突然破窗而入，露出狰狞的牙齿，让我心惊胆战：那你呢？你无非是拿我当挡箭牌，仿佛你可以逃脱自我审视！我问：你到底是谁？法镭哈哈大笑：你臆造了我，居然不知道我是谁？！

2017年1月28

带着它往这边来

朱朱

　　如今已经没有必要以二元论来谈论古典和现代了,古典与现代之间的关系可以在个人这里得以重构。对我而言,以往的所有诗歌文本都是传统,我坐在书桌边,先读上一段李商隐,再读上一段佩索阿,并没有发生什么排异性的反应。曼德斯塔姆那个阿克梅派的定义"对世界文化的怀念",如今其实是一种日常活动,烦恼和疑虑来自于我们企图再一次将古典与现代、东方与西方对立起来或者封闭成两个系统。当我这么说的时候,似乎在规避历史性的思考,但我确认诗性的实质或核心并无二致,并且视每一次具体的写作本身为思考的展开。

　　转化古典的能力取决于个人的认知深度和实践能力。对于我而言,"虚实相间","意在言外",这样的传统写作法则,现在才真正地开始生效。它们改变着我整个的写作形态,并且将我带向某种表达的自由,而这种自由是在我处理当代命题时感知到的。有一个常见的判断错误,就是但凡题材上涉及了古代,或使用着古旧的意象,便会被认为是新古典主义。其实大部分这类诗歌都与古典精神以及趣味无关,只是作者无力对当代发言的证据罢了。苏东坡临死的时候说"著力即差",你一旦刻意强调什么,提倡什么,往往表明你其实虚弱和狭隘。

　　不过,也存在这样的可能,即使我们千方百计地想成为一个世界主义者,但我们最终仍可能是一个一望而知的中国人,确实有什么东西会通过血液或无意识流传下来。其实说来说去,这是一个主体的焦虑问题,这当然是因为自现代以来,我们就面临了文化主体的分裂和异化。置身于这样的语境之中,我们更不能把传统看成任何浮在表面上的花样,那只会把我们的路越走越窄。传统不是召唤你向它那儿去,而是希望你带着它往这边来。你去往它那里,它就是一个巨大的黑洞。你设法带着它来,它就是照亮隧道的手电筒。

注:本文由作者依据 2015 年《中国新诗百年论坛之一:新诗百年与古典传统》的发言整理而有所修补。论坛发言原载于《扬子江诗刊》2016 年第 1 期。此处标题为作者新加。

书已读完
——记一个梦，代替为风诗刊写的创作谈

宋炜

　　和以往的梦不一样，这是一个出现在假寐中的场景。但和以往一样，他还是坐在那儿读书，读完后起身合上书卷，悻悻然摔门离去。

　　由于他阅读的速度太快，一目十行，而翻动书页又尤其迅疾，往往带动那些字，把它们从纸页上一个个抛出，凭空消失。经常一本书被他一读，就成了一册白纸。幸好我有过目不忘之能，并且都先于他早早读过了，一旦有人再想阅读时，只得请我再把它凭记忆复读一遍，才让那些消失的字得以重新出现在纸页上。

　　这次依然如此。我放下格兰凯恩杯，绕过餐桌，拿起犹有他手温的书，展卷之下，一遍惨白。

　　明天肯定还会有人来借阅还本书。我决定用趁热补全它来下我杯中的威士忌。这种经常性的重读其实甚是无趣，只是某一次当我听到了一阵来自那些字之间的抱怨后，才发现有一个更为隐秘的世界存在于一个虚空之中，也就是人们平常所说的"字里行间"，但又不全是——其实还远远不止。当然这样更好，我可以在重读之时旁听到一些多出来的对话。此际，那些低语又出现了——也许是因为多喝了两盎司，我把书中两个男女的一次欢爱提前了，而他们并不同意，说他们当时还没有原谅对方，不会在那种情形下行房。当然，紧接着，提前勃发的欲望令他们立刻又双双同意说会原谅我的孟浪，不过，我得为后面的情节负责：如果那时他们就原谅了对方，就再不会出现在那之后才上场的一个以后会很关键的人物了，他正是那场发生在他们之间的误会的破解者，这样一来，我就活生生扼杀了

一条性命，让一个有大好前途的角色胎死腹中。

　　我不由大吃一惊。于是我马上放下那本重读到中途的书，旋即找到一堆真正的白纸，把它们装订成册，然后双手捧着，用双眼死盯着它。对的，不是读，是盯，因为它天生是一张白纸。但慢慢地，一些字出现在上面，先还全是零碎，字与字之间的组合毫无意义，很快，就有了上下文关系，一座城市和几条街道凭空建起，一些人物不请自来，更多故事自动展开，如果我不是听见敲门声放下这本新的盯了一半的书的话，那个故事绝对不会中止。

　　我开了门，是他，那个一目十行的快读者。他折返了回来，不无兴奋地说：既然所有书卷都已读完，他决定自己写了。我说：不劳你费心了，我已先于你从一个读者变成了作者。当然，很快，你又会把我写的书或你自己写的书——如果你非写不可的话——读完。书总是会被读完的，而那个藏在字里行间的世界也将消失在我们的目光再次（没有再次了）到达之前。

　　于是他再次愤然摔门而去，响动巨大，把我从假寐中惊醒。

2016-11-29，零时刚过，于重庆袁家岗

"人世经停夕光片刻"

——略读韩博《飞去来寺》

蕨弦

从收入诗集《借深心》的《北之西》（2002）、《浅世界的慢旅程》（2003—2004）等系列开始，韩博的作品呈现出明显的空间意识，诗歌场景在不同城市间迅速地切换，世界的"多异"（Divers，谢阁兰的异域情调论中至关重要的概念）纷至沓来。与此同时，一种日后被他广泛采用的写作模式——因旅行的见闻而发，融感怀与奇思于短制之内，再将短诗缀连、结构成整体——也逐步成型。延续着这种写法，韩博在最新的诗集《飞去来寺》里绘制了三轴画卷：《中东铁路》（2011），顾名思义，是沿着那条沙俄时期兴修的要道展开的社会调研与历史追溯，舷窗外剧变的**风物**勾起的宏大叙事构成了组诗关注的焦点；《第西天》（2009）源自作者赴美参加爱荷华国际写作计划的经历，绝大部分诗作都在大洋彼岸写就，东土的访客遭际西域的时空，竟商略出另一片洞天，这大概是其题中之义；标题被用作书名的《飞去来寺》（2003—2013）其实尚未完成，恐怕也不可能真正地完成了，它并非仅是某段旅途的记录，而是一次次往返去来的集合，从某种意义上说，作者是想通过它们书写作为人生之隐喻（"人生天地间，忽如远行客"）的总体的旅行，当然，这丝毫不妨碍每首诗的处理又都各具匠心。

空间感的凸显，暗示着人与外部的关系进入了一个新的阶段。《飞去来寺》作于韩博三十岁到四十岁之间，在这人生中多劳的时节，生活不可避免地被无尽的人事、陌生的时空所侵占。对于一位迫近不惑之年，仍在写作和生活的双轨上行进着的长跑者而言，身处的场景既是灵感生发的基点，一个挥之不去的前提，又是检验想象与现实的契合度的场所。正因为此，在书末那篇辞义深切的跋里，韩博才将生活图景的拓展指认为近些年的写作得以为继的缘由。这或许能够解释一个值得深思的现象：过去数年间，韩博的同侪们相继写下了一系列体量庞大、文体与情思俱佳的"记游诗"，在我目力所及的范围内，有蒋浩的《游仙诗》、张尔的《壮游图》、胡续冬的诗集《旅行/诗》等等。人近中年，阅历的增长同步于技艺的精进和心性的成熟，而"记游诗"恰好提供了一种施展诸种抱负的形式。当然，这也意味着，诗之漫游在他们那里绝不仅仅局限于物理空间。

上世纪末，在将90年代的诗作结集付印时，韩博曾以"十年的变速器"之名提示其中牵涉到的种种心智的变化与风格的转型，似乎历经了十年的磨合后，曾经的少年人已谙熟语言的机括，也习得如何应对世事的消长盈虚，正准备装点行囊，朝下一站进发。虽是一份不无怀旧色彩的自我陈词，却依然难掩对未卜前景的期待。不知是出于偶然，还是一种划分时段的偏好或惯例，《飞去来寺》也是十年诗作的汇编，且"变速器"的意象又无形之中契合了新千年以来韩博的诗里普遍的行游经验，因此可以说，《飞去来寺》也装置着一个"十年的变速器"，但从隐喻的角度看，这种"变速"不再指向长时段内的演进过程，而是细化为微观层面的随机应变。在"社会—历史—语言"的风景中，如何换挡变速，或常速驾驶，对对象亦步亦趋，或拉开一段"安全距离"以便审度，或加速冲破固有的藩篱和隔阂，时时考验着作者的智慧。这样的写作不惟是快意的宣泄，更蕴含着协调错位的身心，联动迥异的社会身份，刺激老化的语言，沟通不同的时空，进而建立"某种有机整体的图式"（《要有光，就有了光头圆脑作僧看》）的潜能。

《中东铁路》正是一次串联历史与当下图景的尝试。我们知道，中东铁路原是横贯欧亚大陆的西伯利亚大铁路在中国境内的一段，其北部干线西起满洲里，东至绥芬河，来自莫斯科的列车经由它前往远东大港海参崴，其南部支线则从哈尔滨一直伸展到旅顺，联结起黑吉辽三省。上个世纪前半期，中东铁路的管辖权辗转于不同政权之间，它的流变如同东北近现代史的缩影：十九、二十世纪之交，沙俄为控制远东修筑了这条铁路；日俄战争以后，大日本帝国将其南下的支线收入囊中；十月革命爆发，工兵苏维埃受列宁之命在枢纽城市哈尔滨夺权；一九二〇年代，长春以北的路段一度由中苏共同运营；东北易帜次年，响应"革命外交"的张学良制造了著名的"中东路事件"；满洲国时期，苏联又将北满铁路卖给日本扶植的政府……相对于既定的轨道，历史的走向固然充满了变数，但不断提速的列车终会将纷争甩在身后。如今，剥离了历史的站台重新被抛掷给北方广漠的虚无，沉默地"杜撰土地的半生"（《时间的卧铺》）。由此，我们不难理解诗中弥漫的"丢失时间"的恍惚感，它揭示的是历史叙事与现实触感之间的疏离，而韩博的写作可以被视为衔接二者的甬道。

鼎革以后，社会主义工业化带来的新变成为了有关中东铁路的叙述不可分割的一部分。在铁路穿过的工业区，楼群拔地而起，工厂喷吐黑烟，机器昼夜作业，快进的时间造就了标准化的场景："主义的/速度肿胀：卸下大同，/运走旧社会与不同。"（《新县城》）。坐落于铁路附近的大庆油田大概也是这般景象，《野鸭与磕头机》一诗很好地还原了那种速度感：

车窗：默念湍急。
平原的湍急，野鸭
下蛋的季节，磕头机
与王进喜默念时不我与。

冻土保温的如画的热的闷墙
湍急：火车捉轨，火车捉鬼。

车窗：将来湍急。
将来：匮乏时代的
车窗：愤怒解决方案。

季节驯育的野鸭
只为湍急的平静下蛋。
石油的平静从未歇脚。

车过大庆，鬼撞心的乘客
庆幸野鸭：无心的逃票者，
彼此乱投彼此，时不我与。

伴随着列车的行驶，自然风光（平原和下蛋的野鸭）、工业景观（不舍昼夜的磕头机，亦即抽油机）与历史记忆（"中国贫油论"的破灭和铁人精神的涌现）紧密地交织在一起，窗景的湍急和"时不我与"的紧迫相互呼应，落实到语言层面，表现为错落的短句营造出的跳跃的节奏。但另一方面，不同"风景"之间又彼此角力着，诙谐的野鸭消解了王进喜与磕头机背后波澜壮阔的叙事，工业文明架构的世界则将野鸭社会化为"无心的逃票者"，由此，三者被共同置入一出"匮乏时代"的戏剧内，高速而盲目运行着，"彼此乱投彼此"。毫无疑问，《野鸭与磕头机》具有一种反思的意味，这一维度也是我们理解《中东铁路》里其他诗作时不可或缺的。二十世纪初期，列车载着马列主义由中东铁路驶入中国，它们轰鸣的汽笛声如同对工农们的号召："蒸汽自西天来，/蒸汽手挽云的剪纸/觉民行道"，但经历了百年间的种种变革后，赤色的承诺最终落空了，徒留"农妇/攥紧钱袋与零存整取的半生的汗的畏途。"（《大杀器》）韩博的跋里提到，他曾在车过哈尔滨时看到筑路工人们拉开巨大的横幅，向雇主讨薪，车窗外讽刺的画面此后无疑发展为了组诗的隐秘动机之一。

如果说《中东铁路》侧重社会问题的勘探和历史情境的想象，那么《第西天》则专注跨文化体验的传递和语言形式的探索，准确来说，是专注异域之旅在母语内的对应、落实和转化。茱萸在分析张尔的《壮游图》时谈到过当代的"记游诗"里"风景"的双重性：某些意象一方面关涉到具体的景观，另一方面也是对文本样态的隐喻。换言之，作者的肉身虽在现实世界游历，但诗中的"壮游"却可能是"心智在修辞层面、语言在探索层面的冒险"（《语言的幽潭，或坎普美学》）。这用以描述《第西天》同样有效，为了言说他者，必须改造自我的认知与语言装置，参照韩博的阐释，作为主体的"东"和作为客体的"西""彼此端详，彼此甄别，彼此完善和拆毁"（《要有光，就有了光头圆脑作僧看》），从而二者均得以深化，所以韩博的美国之行更多地发生在文学乃至文化层面。此外，我们还知道，在当代诗歌的坐标系里，韩博往往被定位为一个极端的语言试验者，其近作大都篇幅精简，句法灵动，好为奇语，多有化用、拼贴、戏仿、谐音、双关之处，方寸之间压缩了丰富的语义，考验着汉语的承载量及柔韧性。《第西天》的书写自然延续了上述特质，且看《第二十三天》是如何经营的：

  北风野餐落木，
  山谷夺胎换骨。
  黄约翰参禅，参差

鸡虫一片：哎噢哇。

不难想见，这首诗大概取材自旅居生活的片段，但在具体处理时，却有高于日常的诗学和文化深意。"哎噢哇"不仅暗合了一片鸡虫的叫声和参禅时幡然醒悟的状态，更是韩博彼时身处的 Iowa 的谐音，根据胡续冬的阐释，这一微妙的联结使异国的语境和"东亚的自然神韵、精神旨趣"被整合到同一平面内（《宇宙是扁的：中国当代诗歌中的异域旅行写作》①）。而山谷句一语双关，既写北风卷地、山谷骤变之貌，又暗指黄庭坚"夺胎换骨"的诗法。《冷斋夜话》引山谷之语："不易其意而造其语，谓之换骨法；规模其意而形容之，谓之夺胎法。"均是因袭前人之意而能以故为新。如此看来，《第二十三天》的次行不啻为首行的注脚。北风起兮、落木萧萧原本是古典诗词里程式化的场景，了无新意，但"野餐"一词竟以郊游的闲适扭转了已沦为俗套的愁苦，这大概能够归入"换骨"之列。同时，通过这句指涉诗歌自身的双关语，诗艺的自觉凸显出来，诗作也因此获致了"元诗"的色彩。

　　《第西天》中最为常见的技法是挪用旧体诗词的章句，在此基础上略加变动，剪裁拼贴，镕铸出新的诗行，若仍要比对山谷的诗法，或许算是"点铁成金"在当代诗语境中的延伸。当然，这绝不是说韩博的诗作要高于被他点化的原作，二者分属于不同的系统，草率的比较无助于把握它们各自针对的问题。事实上，在将打乱后的古典诗词与当代情境对接时，韩博也为前者注入了波普艺术式的戏谑，使诗歌的美学取向发生整体的偏转。举《夜行》的一段为例：

　　无边落木超速，萧萧下，中年危机月黑风高。
　　车灯醉里挑，楚楚动人衣冠的危机推杯换档。
　　安得广厦千万间，众鸟欣有托，露水俱欢颜？
　　安得便携式化工厂采阴补阳，丹炉磕碰心房？

稍有古典诗词阅读经验的读者，不难从中辨认出《登高》、《破阵子·为陈同甫赋壮词以寄之》、《茅屋为秋风所破歌》、《读山海经》等名篇的断片，但经过韩博的编排，杜甫的沉郁也好，陶潜的冲淡和辛弃疾的慷慨也罢，都在插科打诨般的氛围里脱落了，这些诗句被肢解、重组为对都市夜生活的描摹，诗之本事或许无从考证，但显然中年的虚无和欲望才是它们围绕的核心。附带一提，韩博不仅承袭了黄庭坚的诗法，也颇受其生新瘦硬的诗风影响，而为韩博推重的萧开愚同样师法山谷，除此二人外，不同程度地分享着山谷诗——放大了讲也可以说是宋诗——特质的当代诗人还有不少，我们似乎能在新诗中勾勒出一条具有宋诗风貌的脉络。当然，这仅是一家之言，也不在文章的讨论范围之内了。

与紧扣一条线路或一段旅途的《中东铁路》和《第西天》不同，《飞去来寺》的行程覆盖了多国多地，时间跨度约为四年，因此，这组诗没有围绕一个具有统摄性的问题展开，而是呈现出开放的、去中心化的结构，诸种差异的经验和处理方式都被囊括进来。这并不意味着《飞去来寺》里对风景的眺望缺乏问题意识（事实上，观看总是不可避免地预设了某个视角），只是随着漫长旅程的延展，需要应对的风景日新月异，不可能将它们化约后归于几个固定的主题之下（这种写作的处境也是在世的处境），但毫无疑问，组诗里的风景联动于观看者的心绪，《海的侍者》一诗很好地演绎了二者之间的关系：

他被大海拒之门外。

光秃秃的北海，拣选硌脚的路石
砌一座电影院，反锁海燕与翻飞，
淤泥滩与十七岁的狗诅咒的海鸥。

爱丁堡城外的迷宫，整个下午：
快进键尝试淹死主人公。中年
是冒名顶替者的单身牢房，他
攥紧栏杆：乌云走漏的暴风光。

首行的"拒之门外"迅速制造了大海与人的分离；紧接着，作为回应，临眺者也在第二节里以"电影院"的比喻将大海对象化了，海燕、海鸥与淤泥滩都被"反锁"在银幕之中；第三节的"单身牢房"既是对中年状态的形容，同时对称于此前的"反锁"带来的压抑感；最终，在诗的结尾，一线天光穿透乌云，使滞重的海景和昏沉的临眺者都获得瞬间的解脱。"海的侍者"的形象或许会令读者联想到史蒂文斯的《基围斯特的秩序观》（The Idea of Order at Key West）里临海而歌的女人，她使混沌的海洋在她的歌声或者说创造中获得了自我和秩序。《海的侍者》虽与史蒂文斯的诗作有着迥异的语境和意图，但其中的大海同样经历了一个被观看者重塑、赋义的过程。带有人工色彩的"电影院"似乎暗示着"主人公"凭栏远望的不再是自然的海景（或许这种纯粹的自然景观从未存在过），而是铺展于他内部摄影棚的心象。按照柄谷行人的观点，风景看似客观存在于外部，其实与主体的认知模式息息相关，它是"通过对外界的疏远化，即极端的内心化而被发现的"，"只有在对周围外部的东西没有关心的'内在的人'（inner man）那里，风景才能得以发现。"（《日本现代文学的起源》）。不考虑其背后的理论架构而简单地套用这一观点的话，韩博描绘的种种风景实际投射了他不断变动的内部世界，在此意义上，记游文学也兼具着个人精神史的职能。

旅行和生活还在继续，对它们的记录和重思亦复如是，因此《飞去来寺》迟迟没有最终完成，许多诗作从初稿到改定都跨越了十年，而有待更长久的锻打之作或许还尚未被收录。另一方面，在变速器的持续运转中，二者也逐渐获得了同一，这不仅是因为漫游构成了作者生活经验的有机组成部分，更因为尘世生活固有的羁泊之感被游历激发、调动出来了。《车窗外》一诗里，韩博如此书写落日时分停靠于小站的列车："人世经停夕光片刻"。通过将"列车"替换为"人世"，旅行和生活的同构性被揭示出来，更进一步，抽象的"光"则可被视作自然、内面、历史、社会、文化各个层面的风景的象征，它点燃了观景者栖身的车厢，逼促着内外关联的发生。

最后，我想回到组诗的标题，亦是诗集之名，来结束这篇短文。"飞去来"三字对应于作者在各国间的穿梭，不难理解，但末了的"寺"却为读者留出了充足的阐释空间：它所喻指的物质实体，应是乘客搭载的交通工具；它所唤起的参禅的遐想，与韩博暗含机锋的诗语相互印证；甚至，作为避世之所，它还暗示着旅行乃是跳脱樊笼的良机；等等。而我则偏爱一种多少有些玄乎的解释：这"寺"既是一个同步于风景的增长、不断向内搭建的幽微空间，也是风景赖以生成的机制里关键的一环，《车厢外》当中因夕光的插入而骤然敞开的内部是它的诸种变体之一，所有记游之作最终都会落足于这一空间的构筑。

2016年9月4日完稿于沪上复旦
2017年1月略作修改补充

①胡续冬,《宇宙是扁的:中国当代诗歌中的异域旅行写作》,《诗东西》创刊号2010年。

作者简介:蕨弦,1993年生。青年诗人,兼事批评。现于复旦大学中文系攻读现当代文学硕士。诗歌、评论见于《诗刊》《上海文学》《天涯》《飞地》《上海文化》等刊物,并入选多种选本。辑有诗集《夙愿的外观》与《告别放映室》。曾获北京大学"未名诗歌奖"、复旦大学"光华诗歌奖"、南京大学"重唱诗歌奖"、DJS诗东西颁发的"胡适青年诗人奖"等奖项。

Re-reading Hu Shi
重读胡适

Ming Di

From 1915-1916, a group of Chinese students in the United States were engaged in heated debate on whether everyday plain speech (vernacular language) should be used in poetry writing. Hu Shi 胡适 (1891-1962), attending Columbia University then, started writing free verse, allegedly influenced by the *Poetry* magazine in Chicago. He published "A preliminary proposal for literary reform" in the prominent journal *New Youth* (La Jeunesse) in China in January 1917, followed by eight poems in the February issue. He returned to China in July 1917 to promote literary revolution and became one of the most important intellectuals during the May Fourth New Cultural Movement of 1919, which demanded democracy and freedom. In October 1919, he published an essay titled "On New Poetry". In 1920, the first anthology of New Poetry was published, followed by Hu Shi's own collection of New Poetry, Book of experiments. A hundred years later we are still writing New Poetry and experiment with it, for better or worse.

Today, all schools of poets in China, left and right, governmental or independent, unanimously consider January 1917 as the beginning of our current tradition of avant-garde poetry. And Hu Shi is acknowledged as the first poet of New Poetry, and his first poem in the 1917 publication, "Butterflies", as the first New Poem in China. But very few people like this butterfly poem; and nobody takes him as a great poet because most of the poems in his first book resemble the "Butterflies". I'm not motivated to translate it either but will just give a basic idea here: "Two yellow butterflies take off as a pair. / One suddenly returns from the sky / leaving the other one alone in despair / with no more desire to further fly".

What Hu Shi considered revolutionary in this poem was a break away from the tradition of "one poem one rhyme" by alternating a-b-a-b, a Western pattern. But it sounds like a nursery rhyme today. So I took the standard view of regarding him as a poor poet in the preface of *New Cathay – Contemporary Chinese Poetry* (Tupelo Press, 2013). But three months after the anthology was published, I saw Hu Shi's *Diaries As Overseas Student* (Chinese edition, Taipei: Shanghai Bookstore Press, 1937) and was surprised to find his other poems completely different, especially a long one written on July 22, 1916, a month before he wrote the "Butterflies". I would regard this as his first true New Poem, and this is what his New Poetry meant to be.

> Reply to Old Mei – A poem of plain speech
> (答梅觐庄——白话诗)
>
> Days are getting cool, people are less busy,
> Old Mei starts a fight and accuses Hu Shi
> of being too ridiculous in saying
> that "Live literature is what China needs"
> that "Writing must be in vernacular speech!"
> Who says there are live and dead words?
> Isn't the vernacular too vulgar?
> ...
> Old Mei complains, while Hu Shi laughs out loud.
> Cool down comrade, how can you talk so loud
> with such an out-dated tone?
> Words may not be old or new, but definitely dead
> or alive.
> Ancient people say Yu, we say Yao (to desire).

Ancient people say Zhi, we say Dao (to arrive).
Ancient people say Ni, we say Niao (to pee).
Same words, a little change in the sound.
Why call it vulgar?
Why even argue?
Ancient people say letters, we say characters.
Ancient people hang on poles, we hang on beams.
...
Not only words, but also texts,
dead or alive.
A living text is what you know and can speak about.
A dead text is what you have to translate.
Texts of three thousand years, up and down, living or dead,
who knows how many have been hijacked.
Look at the Shangshu.
It becomes fiction.
Look at Songs of Qingyun.
It becomes drama.
...
Look at the texts of Han Tang,
same as the Latin that you're learning.
...
How can there be people so stupid
as to not in love with the living beauty
but hugging the ice-cold skeleton.

Old Mei jumps up: This is absurd!
If what you say is true,
all peasants are poets.
...

Days are getting hot, people are busier.
Old Mei plays with ink, becoming angrier.
But revolution of texts involves both of us.
I dare not argue, nor dare to ignore.
I have to speak out. Not speaking out is not a way out.
Don't you dare laugh
at a poem of plain speech. It beats

a hundred books of South Society texts.
(excerpt from a longer poem)

This was a declaration of free verse in vernacular language. South Society (1909-1923) mentioned at the end of the poem was a poetry club that Mei Jinzhuang (Old Mei) belonged to at that time, where most of the poets were writing in old, bookish Chinese.

While most of Hu Shi's published poems are short and simple, "Reply to Old Mei" has 106 lines divided into five parts, and it is not only long but much more interesting with a citation of major literary works in Chinese history and his critical view of them. It's much freer with irregular lines (vs. the ridged 5 or 7 words per line of the old Chinese poetry). It's charged with anger but also with humor, collaged with different texts – remarks from Mei Jinzhuang and other people and his own counter remarks. In today's standard, it may be seen as hybrid writing with some parts clearly more poetic, and some parts as prose (because poetry can only be lyrical and/or narrative but not debating /argumentative, which belongs to essays, according to the old definition.)

In November 2013, I wrote an essay to correct my previous comments on Hu Shi and called for a "Re-evaluation of Hu Shi". Chen Jun 陈均 (1974-), a poet and poetry critic in Beijing, responded with an essay in the same month saying that it might be a fresh look into the history, but this poem was previously used as "background materials" only, not as a poem. He tried to support me by saying that this poem could be seen as doggerel (打油诗) and Hu Shi's *Book of Experiments* contained some other doggerel poems, and other prominent poets in the 1920s and 1930s of China also wrote doggerels. I would like to argue that doggerels in Chinese history are usually short and funny, but this poem is substantially long and serious, even though it's funny at the same time.

Was Chinese New Poetry born in the U.S.?

Literally so. Hu Shi was in the U.S. from 1910 to June 1917 with scholarships from the Boxer Indemnity Grant – first at Cornell studying agriculture, but he changed to philosophy and literature and then moved to New York City for his PhD in philosophy at Columbia. It was a period of time with great changes. Qing Dynasty was overthrown in 1912, replaced by the Republic of China. The temporary president Sun Yatsun was replaced by the first president of the country, Yuan Shikai, then Yuan died in 1916. World War I broke out in 1914.

On this side, new movements of poetry were taking place in the U.S. ... Hu Shi wrote "Eight don'ts" and published them in the *New Youth* journal in October 1916 in Shanghai, with no response. He made it into an essay with a new title, "A preliminary proposal for literary reform", and published it again in New Youth in January 1917, when the journal was relocated to Beijing, and this time he received an enormous response. Here is some of what he proposed then: Don't write things that say nothing; don't be sentimental; don't use clichés; don't avoid slang or colloquial words. It may look similar to the Imagist manifestos, but he was studying Shakespeare, Tennyson and Browning. His diaries show that he was also reading Chinese classical philosophy and literature and drawing strength from there.

The most "revolutionary" poem of the Literary Reform has been buried in the author's diaries. I'm not even sure if it's politically correct to dig it out, the poem that's written in the U.S. not published in China. But if we take it as poetry, not only will the beginning of New Poetry be dated one year earlier, 1916, and Hu Shi's reputation will change a great deal, but also it will help us define what is New Poetry in China, and how it has evolved to what it is today. Wasn't Hu Shi promoting free verse and plain spoken language? Then why didn't he include in his first poetry collection the poem that's clearly free verse in spoken language? I've found some clues in his diaries. Mei Jinzhuang, a literature major at Harvard, laughed at this poem as "not a poem" "with no rhymes or refined language or crafts at all". The other Chinese students laughed at it too: "It's a total failure". Hu Shi defended himself in the dairies: "It's a half-joking, half-serious experiment of verse in vernacular language. It might be worthless, but it's important in my personal history of writing . . . It's a satire".

"Reply to Old Mei" is informative and persuasive with historical views of the changes in Chinese language and literature. It has a kind of irony that's lacking in most of the poetry in the first five decades in New Poetry. It's carefully crafted with a balanced structure. It's direct, funny and dramatic. It's not sentimental – most of the poems in the 1920s of China were too sentimental and empty. Regarding Mei's accusation of no rhymes, I can see rhymes throughout the entire second part:
xiao, diao, dao, yao, dao, niao, liao, nao, hao,
diao, miao, jiao, mao, zao, bao, kao and hao,
although fewer in the other parts. But who says free verse needs rhymes?

Does a poem need to be published to be a poem? If so, and if the "Reply to Old Mei" is not considered a poem because it's not published, then what about the first two poems by his fellow poet Chen Hengzhe, which did get published in the Overseas Students Quarterly in 1916?

Chen Hengzhe 陈衡哲 (1890-1976) came to the U.S. in 1914, first attending Vassar College, then the University of Chicago. She returned to Beijing in 1920 and became the first woman scholar and professor in China. While in the U.S., she supported Hu Shi's literary reform by writing poems and short stories in the vernacular language. In November 1916, she published two poems in the U.S.-based Overseas Students Quarterly, and in May 1917, her first short story appeared in the same magazine. In 1918, she published more poems and short stories in the New Youth journal. Today, she is commonly considered as the first woman writer in Chinese modern history, arguably the first fiction writer before the literary giant Lu Xun, who published his first short story in 1918, a year after hers. The question is whether literature published in diaspora magazines counts as part of the Chinese literary cannon. If publication anywhere in the world counts, she would be the first poet of Chinese New Poetry. But here comes, again, the question of what is New Poetry. I will reproduce her two poems below, along with my translations:

月

初月曳轻云,
笑隐寒林里；
不知好容光,
已映清溪底。

Moon

Through a thin cloud a new moon climbs up,
then disappears with a cold falling leaf;
but its radiant face reflected in the stream
stays in the clear water and won't leave.

风

夜闻雨敲窗,
起视月如水；
万叶正乱飞,
鸣飙落松蕊。

Wind

At night I hear the rain on my window.
I get up and see moon light, a water fall.
Leaves fly around, soaring, and knock
on the pine trees. The young cones fall.

On the surface level, she followed the traditional form of "Five-word quatrain" with the typical 0-a-0-a rhyme scheme. Since Hu Shi never specified whether New Poetry should rhyme or not, plus there was a strong sentiment to stick to the rhyming systems, these two pieces could pass as New Poems. Hu Shi praised them and recorded them in his diaries, but he never took them as the first New Poetry, because he had published similar semi-new poems in the same diaspora magazine in 1914, especially the one titled "Big Snow". A true New Poem should be something like 'Reply to Old Mei', without constraints of how many words in each line and how many lines in each stanza, or the tonal patterns (平仄) in each line and the 'contrasts' (对仗) in each two lines, etc.

What's New in New Poetry?

Confucius says "day by day make it new" (through Ezra Pound's translation); Hu Shi was experimenting with something new every year. His literary experiment involved translation as well, using different types of Chinese from old to new. In 1914, he translated Browning's "Epilogue to Asolando" and Byron's "The isles of Greece" in the ancient language style of Qu Yuan (343–278 BCE). Later in the same year, he visited Boston and Concord and translated Emerson, but this time in a much freer style:

They reckon ill who leave me out;
  When me they fly, I am the wings;

> I am the doubter and the doubt,
>   I am the hymn the Brahmin sings.
> – from "Brahma" by Ralph Waldo Emerson

> 弃我者，其为计拙也。
> 背我而高飞者，不知我即其高飞之翼也。
> 疑我者，不知疑亦我也，疑我者亦我也。
> 其歌颂我者，不知其歌亦我也。

He called this "prose"; we call it free verse today. The language is classical sounding, but it suits this poem very well, tight and powerful. In July 1915, he wrote a poem in English about the Statue of Liberty in New York, implicating his literary reform in term of ideas, language and form. "Crossing the harbor" begins with, "As on the deck half-sheltered from the rain / We listen to the wintry wind's wild roars", and ends with, "And my comrade whispers to me, / There is 'Liberty'!" Except a few words, it's a short poem of free verse with the clear language that he was looking for in Chinese. I'm translating the whole poem into Chinese here:

> 《穿过港湾》
>
> 甲板上半遮挡着雨
> 我们听见冬天的风在狂野吼叫，
> 听见缓慢的波浪撞击大都会港岸；
> 我们搜寻地球之上
> 闪耀的群星
> 它们照亮了巨大黑暗的苍穹，——
> 在那里——
> 在那盛大的辐射球体之上，
> 一盏灯超群绝伦。
> 我的战友向我耳语，
> 看，那里有"自由"！

I wonder why he didn't re-write it in Chinese. It sounds contemporary. It seems that it was through writing free verse in

English that he finally moved to the writing of Chinese free verse. In his later essays, he defined the New Poetry as a new way of writing that started in the summer of 1915, born out of a long debate. So I would take all his writings in 1915 and 1916 as his experiments including his poems in English. Finally in July 1916, he wrote his loud declaration in that unpublished long poem in Chinese "Reply to Old Mei – A poem of plain speech".

Although Chen Hengzhe supported him by publishing two poems of the new language, but not in free verse, what she wrote and published in 1918 was much less restricted. "People say I'm crazy 人家说我发了疯" was a dramatic monologue, with irregular lines, no rhymes, about an elderly patient rambling in a hospital. Influence from Robert Browning? Chinese ancient poets also used dramatic monologue. "River merchant's wife" by Li Bai (701-762) is an example. Was Robert Browning influenced by Chinese ancient poetry? Possibly, especially since he spent much time in Italy. Marco Polo brought scrolls of poetry and painting to Italy. Later on, Tang poetry was introduced to Italy in the 18th Century and became popular in Europe in the mid-19th Century. Browning had a Chinese friend who was a poet. But Li Bai's influence, if any, needs further study. Since the Chinese students who were enrolled in American colleges were also reading classical Chinese poetry, the seemingly influence from Browning could be from the Tang poets that they were reading. The point is that the early New Poets were inspired by earlier Western poets, as well as earlier/ancient Chinese poets.

Hu Shi won the Corson Browning Prize for his essay "A defense of Robert Browning's optimism". And among the many poets he translated into Chinese, such as Omar Khayyám, Goethe, Heine, Tennyson, Browning, Shelley, Byron, Campbell, Hardy, DH Lawrence, etc. he worked on Robert Browning more and better.

The following is his Chinese translation, apparently better than the original English:

> One who never turned his back but marched breast forward,
> Never doubted clouds would break,
> Never dreamed, though right were worsted, wrong would triumph,
> Held we fall to rise, are baffled to fight better,
>   Sleep to wake.
> – from "Epilogue" by Robert Browning

> 从不转背而挺身向前，
> 从不怀疑云要破裂，
> 虽合理的弄糟，违理的战胜，
> 而从不作迷梦的，
> 相信我们沉而再升，败而再战，
> 睡而再醒。

The following one is probably his best translation:

> Round the cape of a sudden came the sea,
> And the sun looked over the mountain's rim:
> And straight was a path of gold for him,
> And the need of a world of men for me.
> – "Parting at morning" by Robert Browning

> 刚转个湾，忽然眼前就是海了，
> 太阳光从山头射出去：
> 他呢，前面一片黄金的大路，
> 我呢，只剩一个空洞洞的世界了。

The Chinese language here is fresh, even looked at today. I would probably only change three words if it were my translation. Here "the need of a world of men" predicts the situation in his final days, just as "Butterflies" describes his solitude in the early years.

Is the New Poetry movement a Renaissance in China?

Hu Shi has written 300 poems in Chinese, and translated 30 poems and a collection of 17 short stories into Chinese. The Collected works by Hu Shi were published in China in 2003, consisting of 44 volumes, mostly essays and diaries. As New Poetry continued blooming through the 1930s and 1940s, many other poets were very productive and left volumes of New Poetry.

Hu Shi is now remembered as a pioneer of New Poetry, never a major poet, due to his own poor judgment, or the severe attacks from his contemporaries on his more serious experiments, such as the long poem "Reply to Old Mei" and his translation of Byron's "The isles of Greece". He was proud of his translation of Sara Teasdale's "Over the roof", which was talked about excessively in the studies of New Poetry for the wrong reasons. He felt that he discovered a way of translating the iambic into Chinese, which further supported the use of modern Chinese: in classical Chinese each word is one syllable, but in modern vernacular Chinese one word can be 2-3 syllables, creating the stressed and unstressed. By imitating the English iambic lines, he created a new kind of free verse in Chinese. However, I think his translation of Auld Robin Gray (老洛伯) by Anne Lindsay is even better, completely free and with a natural rhythm, and it's one of the best free verse poems in the early Chinese New Poetry.

To paraphrase what Hu Shi wrote in his diaries: his revolution was nothing new, Dante wrote in Italian instead of Latin, Chaucer got rid of the old English, and Martin Luther moved on from the old German. As for the literary revolutions in China: Qu Yuan's poetry was the first revolution, short poems of 5 or 7 words per line were the second revolution, the prose poems of the Han Dynasty (202-220) were the third, the regulated poetry of the Tang Dynasty (618-907) with a strict tonal system was the fourth, the de-regulated Ci of Song Dynasty (920-1279) was the fifth, and the change from Ci to the lyrics and drama of Yuan (1271-1368) and Ming (1368-1644) Dynasties was the sixth revolution. He was merely continuing the spirit of making changes and moving forward.

If we look at the notorious butterfly poem (两只黄蝴蝶) more closely, we will see that it's a "double five-word quatrain" (双绝句):

    xxxxx, xxxxx。a
    xxxxx, xxxxx。b
    xxxxx, xxxxx。a
    xxxxx, xxxxx。b

The regulated five-word quatrains in the High Tang Dynasty are five words per line and four lines per stanza, followed by an optional second stanza. The change to the double quatrains horizontally may look trivial, but the extended lines demonstrate the major changes in language: in modern Chinese a word can be two to three characters, and therefore the new language doesn't fit into the old forms any more. (Also of note is that Hu Shi was the first to use punctuations in Chinese.) More importantly, he revived the old quatrain from the Tang Dynasty and gave it a new shape, the doubled lines.

Hu Shi acknowledged the vernacular language used in ancient poetry. As poetry died out in the Ming and Qing Dynasties, he called for a revival of poetry and revival of vernacular language. Vernacular Chinese has existed throughout history. Li Bai's best known poem, "Quiet night thought", is an example. Li Bai wrote two kinds of poetry, using either classical or vernacular Chinese.

Li Shutong 李叔同 (1880-1942), Hu Shi's contemporary, 11

years older than him, spent five years in Japan studying art and music and returned to China in 1910, the year Hu Shi left China for the U.S. Li and several others brought Western culture to China through Japan, and Li was the first to teach Western painting and music in China. In 1915, he wrote the lyrics for a song, "Farewell", breaking the traditional metrical system of poetry. It was rediscovered in the 1940s and again in the 1980s.

Farewell

Outside the pavilion, along the ancient trail
green grass stretches joining the horizon.
Evening wind blows the willows in the fading tune of a flute
while the sun sets over the mountains and mountains.

At the sky's end, and the ocean's corner
friends are scattered with only a few to hold.
Tonight we drink and exhaust the joys,
then we part and our dreams will be cold.

The original Chinese has alternating numbers of characters /space in each line, with an incredibly amazing pause in the first line of each stanza:

xxx, xxx (a)
xxxxx   (a)
xxxxxxx (b)
xxxxx   (b)

xxx, xxx (c)
xxxxx   (c)
xxxxxxx (b)
xxxxx   (b)

It's rhymed but not in the traditional way. The language is simple and plain, a little bit melancholy, awaking a sense of nostalgia immediately. It's not cutting edge in today's standard, but it was innovative in 1915. The lyric was written under the influence of a Japanese lyricist who re-wrote the lyrics for an American song, but each was independent work. I would love to take this as the first New Poem in Chinese history. However, Li Shutong didn't have a manifesto of literary reform or consciousness of nationwide reform expressed elsewhere, such as in essays. Nor did he influence anyone. The other consideration is: to discuss literary influence from Japan is not politically correct in China, because of the Japanese invasion of China in the 1930s and because of "national pride". It might be for the same reason that Hu Shi's poetry, written in the U.S. and unpublished in China, is never considered as Chinese poetry. Or perhaps I'm oversensitive. It might well be that most poets have not seen "Reply to Old Mei". Personally, I'm not really concerned about where New Poetry was born but how it has evolved. Li Shutong in China and Hu Shi in America were both trying to write a new kind of poetry using plain spoken language, with some ancient elements. It has been noted that Li Shutong's "Fairwell" resembles the poetic style of Fan Zhongyan (989-1052) in the Song Dynasty, which supports the notion that the New Poetry movement in the early 20th Century is a Renaissance in its full meaning.

What's most important and mostly forgotten is that New Poetry is not against the ancient poetry in China, but the classical language (文言文), especially the "eight-legged" language (八股文) that prevailed in the Qing Dynasty (1644-1912), which was becoming more and more rigid and stiff because of the long Imperial Examination System (科举制) from 605 to 1905. The ending of that system and the downfall of the Qing Dynasty made the literary reform possible. As Hu Shi indicated, New Poetry was a renaissance of ancient Chinese poetry, using plain and clear language for the complicated modern life.

Hu Shi was also interested in earlier poetry from the Middle East. He translated Omar Khayyám (1046-1131) so beautifully:

> 要是天公换了卿和我，
> 该把这糊涂世界一齐打破，
> 再磨再炼再调和，
> 好依着你我的安排，把世界重新造过！
> – Rubaiyat #73

It's interesting to notice that the Rubaiyat (鲁拜集) has the same shape as the Tang quatrains, four lines per stanza, and same rhyming patterns. But what's in Hu Shi's Chinese translation is a new music made possible by using modern Chinese with a classical tone. As "Reply to Old Mei" says, "Texts of three thousand years, up and down, living or dead,/ who knows how many have been hijacked". In a positive sense, being "hijacked" can bring changes, something ancient with a new life.

Artistically, "Reply to Old Mei" is quite contemporary with its hybrid writing and collage of various types of texts. It's the traditional "standard" view of what's poetry that makes it non-poetry. I'm even beginning to wonder if *The Book of Songs* edited by Confucius was really the first anthology of poetry in Chinese history. We have *The Book of Mountains and Seas* (山海经) from the ancient time, an epic of 18 volumes about the mythologies, geographies, and polytheistic religions of ancient China. Why has it never been considered as poetry? Is it because of its irregular shape (different numbers of words in each line) and lack of rhyme? What else was filtered by Confucius? According to his standard, "Reply to Old Mei" would never be a poem, ever, despite the fact that there has not been any other writings, not to say poems, that has defended poetry in contemporary China so powerfully and eloquently in the last 100 years.

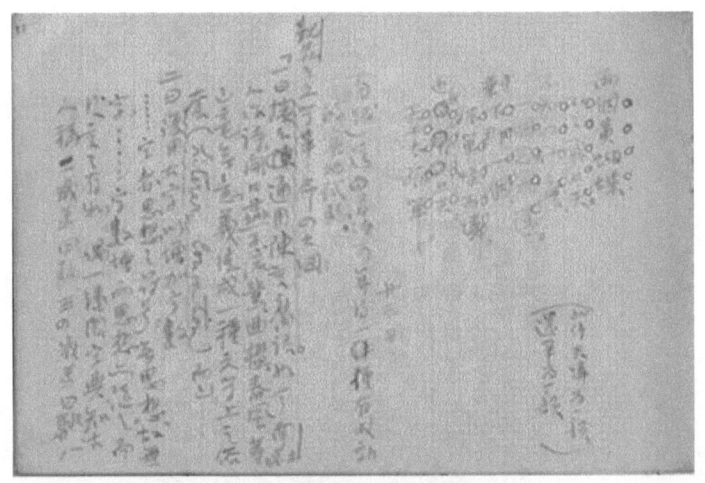

Hu Shi's hand-writing of his "Butterfly" poem.

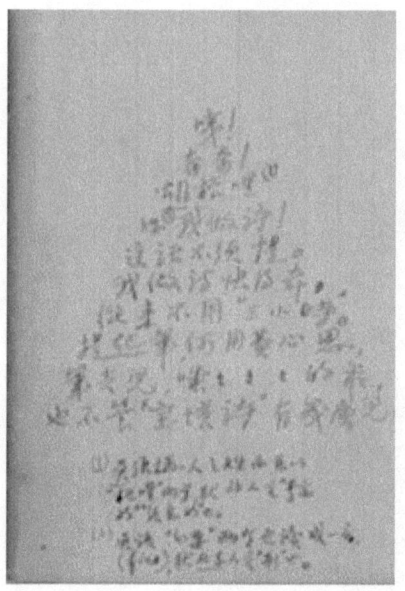

Hu Shi's pagoda poem in his hand writing, which will be discussed in the next issue of FENG.

访谈：敬文东 森子 姜涛 茱萸 等

前言：新诗"日日新"

中国新诗的现代性以胡适1916《答梅觐庄——白话诗》为起源，与新诗的发生同步，40年代达到小高峰，然后似乎出现一个断层，但越来越多的诗人被重新发现，他们的写作延续了现代性脉络，也使新诗各种风格的形成和流变更加清晰。新诗经过百年历程（包括战争年代和各种运动）而多彩多姿，几乎在每一阶段的主流之外，都有求新求变的诗人或诗人群体；先锋一旦成为主流之后，新的创新就会出现。前几年做的一个问卷访谈主要围绕诗人的成长环境、文学启蒙、阅读、写作、风格的形成、流派、外来诗的影响等12个问题。本次问卷是这个跟踪系列的一部分。回答不代表采访人立场，前言也不代表被采访人立场。

中国新诗产生于中西文化和思想观念碰撞的年代。如果没有科举制废除、清朝被推翻，就难以有新诗的发展，没有五四运动也难以推广和继续。孙中山早年赴美国夏威夷、日本、美国旧金山等地，接受了西方文化、基督教、以及革命理念，回国后领导推翻了清朝，1912年建立民国，1919年建立国民党。1915年陈独秀从日本回中国创办新青年杂志，1917年1月将杂志从上海迁到北京。1916-1917年胡适在新青年上两次发表文学改革建议，1917年从美国回国，发起白话诗运动。1917-1922年《新青年》由陈独秀、胡适、周氏兄弟及北大同仁轮流编辑，1919年阵营分化，一路激进，走向社会革命，以陈独秀为代表，一路坚持自由主义立场，以胡适为代表。1921年中国共产党成立，《新青年》曾是引进西方马克思主义和共产主义的重要理论阵地。新文学/新诗从20世纪20年代开始出现左翼和右翼之分，1930年左翼作家联盟成立(1935

年解散)。1949年之后，"左"逐渐成为思想文化与文学的主流。1957-58年反右运动，"右"被命名为反党标志（22年后平反）。当代中国，左右都有标榜自由、思想开明者。早期新诗诗人大多熟悉《四书》《五经》，即使全盘西化，也有传统痕迹。21世纪以来左右都有回归本土传统的愿望，也都有继续接受西方文学的倾向，很难在对待新诗中外资源的态度上辨别，更何况"西方"分有不同国家的不同源流。尽管各种文学主张有合流的趋势，观念不断多元化，但在细处和深处，在诗歌是否应具有教育功能、社会性、道德伦理评判性等等，仍然有主流话语和自由思想之分。但主流和非主流在当今难以界定，或者说不完全由身份来界定，而由审美取向来界定。诗人的身份、立场、观念、写作，属于不同的层面，即使在同一个诗人身上也没有统一性。而"独立"既不是身份也不是立场标榜，而是文本的无畏、不屈从于任何价值标准。这个问卷关注的是新诗发展和演变，以及当代诗的生态环境和人文环境；关注多元文化；关注好诗；关注持续的语言创新和诗学创新。孙中山的逸仙之名是"日新"的广东话谐音，取自儒家经典《大学》的"苟日新，日日新，又日新"，后者正是庞德所翻译的"日日新"原始出处。清朝之后，中国新诗如何"日日新"，是这个系列问卷访谈所关注的核心。（明迪2016年2月于加州）

2016年中国诗人访谈共邀请16位诗人参与，前面八个问题的英文版发表于鹿特丹诗歌节网站2016年8月《中国诗人专号》。现把问卷最后几问合并一起，以中文刊出。

问：与古诗相比，新诗在中国当下处于什么地位？百年了，是否已成为主要的诗歌写作方式？对新诗的批评主要来自新诗写作者还是旧体诗写作者？你认为有哪些批评是合理的？新诗是否已经成熟？以什么为标志？在西方文学和哲学、中国古典文学和哲学、白话新诗的三大影响下，当代诗人近30年是否开辟出新路？有哪些探索？如何接通古典（不同时期）？新诗百年了，当代诗人是守成还是创新？如何创新？是否有重建先锋意识的必要？当代诗人需要颠覆什么？超越什么？或建立什么？

敬文东：中国新文学是全球化在现代中国的终端产品之一。它如果不说是地地道道的西方产物，起码也是以西方文学为参照建立起来的文学样式——西方文学是中国新文学之母。它从一开始，就受到翻译作品的影响；没有翻译，就没有中国的新文学或现代文学，至少不是我们现在看到和熟悉的那种文学样态。从这个角度观察，翻译文学给中国新诗带来的影响可谓正负"交加"，但还不敢说正负"参半"——这样精确的比例并不存在。从正面的角度说，翻译过来的诗歌（主要指欧美诗歌）缔造了新诗的形式观念、构词法则，更重要的或许是：以如此这般的形式观念和构词法则应对慢慢现代起来的中国经验。这致使新诗至少从长相上，和源自农耕生活的古典汉诗相差天壤，判若云泥。但相较于古典汉诗，新诗确实能更好地承载现代中国人的现代经验——这是中国新诗必须感谢翻译文学的原因之一。从负面的角度看，翻译文学主要是给新诗带来了所谓的"翻译腔"，致使新诗远离了中国的文学传统，似乎同汉语从血缘上断绝了关系——这似乎是新诗的题中应有之义。但为应对被迫的全球化，还有"被译介的现代性"（刘禾语），而彻底远离源远流长的自家传统，无论如何不能说是一件让人骄傲的事情，更遑论满意的事情。这正负两方面的情况，自打新诗出现伊始，就得到了注意，甚至受到了重视，许多早期的新诗诗人为此有过深浅不一的反思。闻一多试着为新诗的形式寻找纪律或法则，戴望舒、废名、林庚等人，则试图接通中国古代的抒情传统。但他们的反思和努力也称得上成败交加；以或成或败的眼光看过去，他们的工作似乎都有道理，也很有必要。我的看法是，必须把新诗视作现代性在中国文学方面的终端产品。它之所以出现，本质上，是为了应对现代性在更广泛的角度上的终端产品：个人与垃圾。垃圾在此暂且不论，对于新诗，个人却是逃不掉的话题。个人的本质是孤独，而且是绝对意义上的孤独，无法解决的孤独。因此，新诗无论如何变化，其表达的目标和内容，都必须得到孤独的定义，无论是正面的定义，还是反面的定义。至于大陆中国较长时间在新诗中看似成功地驱逐了孤独，现在的研究者却更倾向于将之视作新诗的逆流,至少也是偏师,是不入流——我当然无条件地同意这个观点。当年,我们的先辈为应对突如其来的现代性,宁愿选择与"母舌"(郭绍虞语)相背离的"翻译腔",也要远离伟大而流畅的抒情传统,既是迫不得已之事,也是很有道理之事,我们有必要对他们持"理解之同情"的态度。如今,新诗已经有了百年"小"传统,今天的诗人应该有底气和自信回视自己的"大"传统,不再惧怕古典汉诗中的消极成分;今天的诗人应该更有能力找到打通古今的道路。无论如何,被废置的宝藏还是宝藏,垃圾只是放错了地方的宝贝。远的不谈,最近三十多年来,很多诗人在借鉴古典传统方面有过很不错的尝试,张枣、赵野、柏桦、萧开愚、桑克、蒋浩等人,都曾奋力杀出血路,为新诗在"翻译腔"之外寻找新路径,拓展新道途。在这里,我想特别提到四川诗人宋炜,一位真正的诗歌隐士,常年隐于酒色,不屑于发表作品,更不理会别人是否理解他的作品。但是,很可能是宋炜而不是别人,才是最近几十年来在打通古今那方面用力最猛者,成就最大者。他一大批暗中在朋友圈子内流传的作品,称得上光彩夺目,令人兴奋。古典精神流溢其间,古色中有现代,现代中有古色,让读者大起不知今夕何夕之感,汉唐风韵和现代风气相杂陈,是真正意义上的打通古今,不仅仅是所谓的化古为今——化古为今恰好是不入流。和宋炜相比,余光中先生几十年前的努力就显得既表面,又肤浅,像快餐,像速成食品,让既不知古也不知今的人拍手叫好。但宋炜只是找到了适合于他自己的道路,事实上还有很多路数可走,就看谁更有好运气了。

森子: 新诗是当代诗歌写作的主要力量,这是无疑的。新诗写作对表现、揭示当代人的精神、生活状况是旧体诗不能比拟的,对当代生活深度、广度的全面探索也是旧体诗所不能及的。新诗是否成熟,也许并不十分重要,关键在于它的创新能力和开放性有多大、多强烈,最美妙的事情莫过于始终处于形成之中。如果没有当代的新诗,谈论古典诗歌便没有现实意义,传统依赖于当代,只有从新诗出发才有可能更好地理解古代传统,新诗与古诗差异越大,其内部的创造力的相似性就越多。也许,继承传统的最好方式之一就是你在熟知它的情况下——能离它有多远。

如果把"守成"看作是对百年新诗写作的研究、总结、再发现，我还是乐意接受的。因为创新并不否定继承已有的传统，我认为传统并不是固化的，而是流动的，处于不断生成变化之中。不应该以静止的眼光看待正在写作中（在路上）的新诗，新诗的道路即在看似不可能中伸向远方。新诗最主要的功能也许就是你不能轻易地规定它。如今，诗人们很少谈论"先锋性"，不是因为"先锋性"不重要，而是与其不停地空谈、宣言、运动，不如踏实地在写作中落实。从中也可以看出诗人写作意识的转变，不再像上世纪 80 年代那样冒进。诗人能够颠覆什么？也许只能颠覆世界，颠覆世界的观念，让月球垮台，乌托邦留产。超越火星，诸如此类的计划，移民梦想，建一座母语的太空城。其实诗人要做的只一件事，无论在梦里梦外——都要自由。

桑克：在中国，新诗没有政治地位（政府报告从来不提，而毛写旧体诗），社会地位很低（大众基本不关心，媒体关注度不仅低而且非常不专业，而高级官员不少写旧体诗，尤其退休之后，因而某些旧体诗又有"老干体"的称谓），文化地位很低（次于建筑电影美术音乐而几与舞蹈相似，旧诗文化地位也不高，虽然《诗刊》的一个奖，新诗是十万块，旧体诗是三十万块），文学地位较低（次于小说报告文学散文戏剧，在这个序列中，旧诗的地位还不如新诗）。

新诗是相对于旧诗概念而成立的。准确地说，现代诗已经成为主要的诗歌写作方式。现代诗比新诗的概念更有意义。对新诗的有效批评主要来自新诗写作者和部分学者。
无效批评主要来自社会（包括部分媒体）。部分旧体诗写作者并不批评新诗，而是瞧不起写新诗的，他们认为新诗根本不是诗。旧体诗有非常出色的诗人，比如陈寅恪、聂绀弩（当年在 850 农场）……不知道翻译成英文会是什么样子。合理的批评很多，比如还应该更加多元化，比如想像力还是应该加强……

新诗成熟，标志是九十年代诗歌。古代诗歌传统对当代写作基本无效，古代诗歌资源对当代写作非常重要，是极其宝贵的文化遗产和灵感来源。本土传统如果是指九十年代诗歌，如果是指更早的西南联大诗歌……那么就继承吧。古体诗和近体诗当然可以写，我小的时候写过三千多首。不过不写也没什么。

姜涛：新诗与旧诗的关系，一直是个争议性的话题，车轱辘式的价值评判，也持续了近百年。其实，新诗与旧诗在现代社会，属于不同的文化系统，旧诗大体上属于文化传承、人文修养、抒怀遣兴的范畴，作者和读者都要比新诗更多。新诗更多是一种纯粹的、先锋的文学，与变化中的，两种游戏可以彼此借鉴、勾连，但毕竟规则不同。谈及新诗的成熟，或许不少读者和批评家希望新诗能变成另一种类型的古诗，有稳定的形式、美学、象征系统，殊不知新诗是20世纪中国文化危机中的产物，"新"或许是它的内在本质，"不成熟"也可作为一种历史性格来看待。1930年代，林庚先生就说：自由诗，是一种紧张精警的文学，而格律诗的风度，则是从容自然。他的理想是兼备紧张与从容，坚持新异、先锋原则的同时，也保有某种宽广、温润的力量。这个看法其实很有启发性，"化欧"与"化古"本来就是新诗内部的一种辩证张力，而传统不单纯局限在词句、风格、意境的层面，古典诗歌背后的人文视野和综合心智，恰恰是可以给新诗以内在的滋养、支撑。

30年来的当代诗歌，已经形成了自身的传统，在提及的三大影响之外，当代中国特定的政治压力和巨大的社会变动，也是该"传统"保持内在活力的一个前提。如果说"创新"是新诗的本质规定的话，那么这个"新"的含义，应该比已经体制化的先锋性、实验性更为宽广，语言的变动联动世道人心的洞察、改善努力，新诗之"新"应体现在一种逐渐成熟的文化创造力之中。

蒋浩：我们不知道新诗何日而终，所以，我看不到她目前究竟出于她的童年还是青年。中国古代传统与当下写作之间的关系很复杂，也很巨大，难以万言，但有一点是可以肯定的，就是语言就是命运，而这种由语言带来的命运既安排的诗人，也安排了诗歌。所以，我们始终有一脉相承和一以贯之的东西，当你必须用中文写作时。至于当代诗人如何传承古代传统，因人而异，但是个值得研究的大课题。

新诗还在发展中，一代人做一代的事，其中既有传承，也有创新。现在基本不提"先锋"这个概念了，因为当代诗和八十年代所说的"先锋"发生了很大的改变，那时候的先锋是一种必须的姿态和必然的策略，而今天不再使用这个词，也许意味着先锋性不仅需要颠覆、超越，更需要建立。颠覆既有的写作范式，这是写作学的基本伦理要求；超越诗歌作为依赖语言或仅仅是语言的艺术，通过个人写作建立一种诗歌和社会、历史等产生广泛关联和深刻摩擦的正在构成诗人新的诗性人格。

郑小琼： 新诗肯定是主要潮流，虽然我在另外一份资料上看到，中国旧体诗创作的人数十分庞大，但是与新诗比起来，影响甚微，近十年来，中国诗歌有一股复古情怀，这种复古情怀不仅体现在旧体创作的诗人增加，年轻人的参与，而在新诗创作中也有呈现。我并不认为是新诗或者旧体诗哪个是"主要潮流"的问题，作为新诗创作者，我个人觉得在新诗创作融入中国传统是一件很值得新诗创作者探索的主题，汉语的优美在新诗中丧失得极多，回过头来看，80年代那一批诗人，比如张枣、柏桦、钟鸣等人的诗歌就有相当好的传统性的东西。在前几十年里，新诗创作者与古体诗创作可能是两个互不干涉与交流的群体，彼此间批评得多，近些年似乎两个圈子的人开始交流，并没有以前那样激烈对抗了。我不认为新诗是成熟了，相反它还在探索时期。如何传承本土古代传统就是一个主题之一。以我自己为例，我花了数年时间重新阅读来中国古代文学创作，我觉得中国魏晋南北朝的赋是一种很意思的文体，它里面的修辞、想象力等有太多东西值得我们关注，古代汉语的优美在新诗慢慢恢复。

茱萸： 新诗在新文化运动以降"现当代文学"体系中，自然是百年来诗体的主要潮流。但是，传承数千年的旧诗传统未绝，依然有很强的生命力，只是大多数新诗写作和研究者出于傲慢和偏见，对此并不足够了解和熟悉。反过来说，对新诗的批评自然主要来自新诗内部，因为当代大多数的旧体诗词写作者并不对新诗这种东西感兴趣；既不了解，那么判断或臆或偏，并不能构成有效的批评。非要说的话，旧体诗词作者通常对新诗的最大批评是，它并没有一个显著的"他律"在起作用，而这种"他律"也主要集中在音韵方案和形式方案上。这样的批评有一定的合理性，这也是新诗一体自诞生以来贯穿始终的内在焦虑。

作为欧美诗歌的中国投射、一种"舶来品"，新诗的方法论和精神气质，和旧诗都相去甚远——即便经由近百年的演变，新诗似乎已沾染上了一些所谓的"本土特质"。旧诗对新诗构成一种什么样的意味，倒一直是新诗史上及近年来创作界持续关注的热点问题，它对有志于在新诗领域中进行创造性劳作的诗人和批评家来说，甚至构成了某种精神上的焦虑，这就是所谓"传统的阴翳"。当代诗人黄灿然写过一篇关于汉语现代诗的文论，题目就叫"在两大传统的阴影下"，这两大传统指的就是在诗歌内部而言的汉语古典诗词传统和欧美现代诗传统。汉语新诗自一百年前诞生伊始，就一直面临着文体合法性建构的焦虑，这种焦虑的来源之一，就是新诗该如何看待和处理与诗词的关系。新诗诞生之初的那三十年，当时的诗人和学者们在这个问题上有过很深入的创作尝试和理论探讨，比如闻一多、孙大雨、卞之琳、废名、林庚、吴兴华、朱英诞等人。在近十多年中，关于这个话题的探讨在新诗界又重新热了起来，不过由于新诗作者们整体而言比较差劲的旧学素养，使这份"重温"显得并没有太多可取之处。

我其实在一定的语境内认同"新诗不是诗"这个看似极端的论断。因为倘若将"诗"定义为传统意义上的"韵文"的话，那么别的先且不论，单在音韵方面，新诗就不具备构成诗之为诗的要件。新诗的音韵问题相对复杂，它所参照的欧美现代诗，除了真正的自由体外，也不是没有格律音韵的要求，只不过这种要求移植在现代汉语中的话，无法得到有效的呈现，单独的押尾韵模式，又使得以双音节词为主的现代汉语诗，在调性和风格上有沦为顺口溜和打油诗的可能。新诗至今没有提出一套具有普遍说服力而又能保证其艺术性的音韵方案。音韵问题而导致的"新诗不成立"说，其实要归因于新诗的舶来特质以及现代汉语本身的特点。正以为如此，我倾向于认为，虽然都叫"诗"，但新旧之间的鸿沟，其实非常大，大到甚至近似于旧诗和小说之间的差别——新诗和旧诗根本就是两种文学体裁，它们可以如小说之于诗词那样沟通精神资源，但无法共享文体特质。在亲缘度上，新诗和旧体的关系远不如新诗和欧美现代诗。Poetry 被翻译成"诗歌"而不是别的什么，实在是前贤们对"遗留问题有多么严重"并无意识的结果。

秦三澍：在当代文学的总体中，新诗的重要性及取得的实绩绝不亚于其他文体；曾有一种说法，认为当代文学中惟诗歌可以进入世界一流的话语体系中，通过对中外诗歌的对照阅读，我觉得这个说法有一定道理。

也正是在这个意义上，我认为新诗自 1990 年代后期以来，加速进入成熟期，至少在写作文本上体现了这一点。至于说，新诗是否建立了与之创作想匹配的批评和研究体系，个人倒是持保留意见。整体上，当代诗的"成熟"或"渐趋成熟"仍亟待更有效的诠释。因而，面对旧诗的诘难，新诗的回应还显得疲软；不过，诘难有时也不需要回应，毕竟这也是新诗不断扫描并克服自身"盲区"的必要途径。

至于当下新诗写作与"古代传统"的关系，我时常所谓的古代诗文传统不当做"传统"而视作"资源"，不是去"接续"或"传承"它，而是将它作为"借鉴"和"征用"的对象，这样才能消除一种传统断裂的幻象带来的焦虑感。而更深一层，也并不是为了刻意消除这种焦虑感，而是因为新诗和旧诗实为两种不同的文体，尽管他们的核心词都是"诗"这个字。但此"诗"非彼"诗"，不可等量观之。

三十年中国当代诗人走出了一条新路，这是确而无疑的事实。至于为何要在"百年"这个节点上选择守成或创新，我感到费解：其一，百年对于新诗而言时间仍太短，远未到"盖棺定论"的时刻；其二，当代诗人每时每刻都应该担起开拓新路、新领域的职责。

"先锋性"的内容随历史语境而变，当下的先锋性绝不类同于八十年代的先锋性。仅就目下而言，如何将对事物的观察和对日常经验的重审纳入到智性的范围，重建一种心智上的高度和宽阔范围，是那些我认为"先锋"的当代诗人们正在做的；"先锋"的另一维度也体现在，他们将对于现代汉语的奇妙可能性的打造，譬如征用古典文学传统的词句或被认为是"非诗"的语汇，锻造一种混杂性的、跨语体的语言景观。

This group interview was conducted in 2016. The English version of Questions 1-8 was published on Poetry International/ Rotterdam web in August 2016. The above is the Chinese version of Questions 9-12 combined, published here for the first time. Below is Question 8 re-printed while 1-7 can be found online: http://www.poetryinternationalweb.net/pi/site/cou_article/item/28080/A-Survey-on-Controversial-Issues-Regarding-Contemporary-Chinese-Poetry

8. What's the status quo of New Poetry (free verse in vernacular language)? After 100 years since Hu Shi started it in 1916, has it become the primary mode of poetry writing in China? What's the relationship between classical poetry and New Poetry today?

Jing Wendong 敬文东: Chinese modern literature has been heavily influenced by Western literature. Wen Yiduo tried to find new metrical system for the New Poetry. Dai Wangshu, Fei Ming and Lin Geng tried to find a way to connect to the Chinese traditional lyricism. But their efforts were half failures. Contemporary poets are trying to find new ways. Hermit Song Wei has some brilliant poems circulating among friends, very exciting poems. What Yu Guangzhong did in Taiwan is too shallow.

Zhang Qinghua 张清华: Although translation of Western literary has brought positive influences, contemporary poets are trying to bring the Chinese traditional elements back into their writing.

Yang Xiaobin 杨小滨: Contemporary Chinese poetry has undoubtedly opened up a variety of new paths. New Poetry has become the main fashion of poetry writing but New Poetry has not achieved the high status like the classical poetry. The poetry of our current time represents the best achievement of New Poetry with the vitality of classical poetry and modern taste.

Zhu Yu 茱萸: If we have to make the comparison, I would say we don't have Tao Qian, Shen Yue or Geng Xin in our New Poetry yet, not to say Du Fu, Li Shangyin or Huang Tingjian. However, New Poetry is so lively, open to endless possibilities.

Chen Jiaping 陈家坪: I think New Poetry is being neglected because it's absent in the school text books. New Poetry is not competing with the classical poetry but to grow out of it.

Sen Zi 森子: Without the New Poetry, it would be pointless to talk about the classical poetry. Whether New Poetry is mature or not is not that important. What's important is that it has the power of self-generating and self-renewal. It's making it new by itself.

Qin Sanshu 秦三澍: Since the 1990s, our New Poetry has speeded up its development. What's lacking is sufficient criticism and research work. Regarding the debate, New Poetry and classical poetry have different traditions. Classical poetry is not a tradition for us to carry on but literary resources for us to use. This is the way to eliminate the anxiety.

Zheng Xiaoqiong 郑小琼: The beauty of the Chinese language is disappearing in the current New Poetry. Looking back at the poetry of the 1980s, poets like Zhang Zao, Bai Hua and Zhong Ming possessed traditional qualities. There are many people writing the classical form of poetry. It's a completely different world, but there is interaction between the two worlds now. I think Fu style from the Wei Jin Southern and Northern Dynasties is very interesting with its rhetoric. The classical beauty is returning to the New Poetry slowly.

Jiang Tao 姜涛: Writing in the classical form is continuation of Chinese culture and therefore there are a lot more practitioners and readers of classical poetry than New Poetry. New poetry (free verse) is a type of avant garde literature in China. It was the product of the cultural crisis in the 1920s. To take the Western influence or the classical heritage has been the tension within New Poetry. "New" should carry a wider meaning than the institutionalized poetry in China.

Sang Ke 桑克: New Poetry has very low social status. Mao was writing classical poetry. Many government officials practice the classical metrical form. Poetry magazine has a poetry award that gives 100000 RMB for New Poetry and 300000 RMB for classical poetry.

A Xiang 阿翔: Chinese New Poetry is in a golden age even though it's marginalized. It has nothing to do with the various kinds of festivals or prizes. It's due to the spirit of "making it new". What's important is to develop a unique voice with validity and competitiveness.

Ya Shi 哑石: Compared to the almost unified outlook of life in classical poetry (of any period of time), New Poetry embodies modern experience which is complexed. Compared to the unified judgment of good or bad in classical poetry, New Poetry is more intricate even though in free verse. I know it sounds like there are many gaps but the gaps nurture unimaginable possibilities for us.

对新汉诗的想象

浅读李森 陈均 西渡 倪志娟 等

IMAGING THE NEW CHINESE POETRY

MING DI

I have imagined Chinese New Poetry to be uniquely "Chinese" attracting Western readers again like the impact of Li Po, Tu Fu and Wang Wei's poetry in the past. I know it's an ambitious anticipation but I've started to collect poems anyway, from poets known and unknown. The key issues are: after a century of free verse writing and interaction with poetry around the world, what is Chineseness now? After three thousand years of Chinese poetry compiling since the *Book of Songs*, what is new? What is good and new? Many Chinese poets have experimented with different forms and languages. What has attracted me is not a pure revival of the ancient form but innovative forms and linguistic dynamics.

During a recent contact with Li Sen 李森 (b1966) from Yunnan province about a joint Ecopoetry project, I started to read his poems and found them extremely interesting and refreshing. For instance,

橘在野　　　orange in wilderness

日出东南　　　sun rises in southeast
橘在野　　　　orange in wilderness
黄在橘　　　　yellow in orange

阳在橘	sun in orange
阴在橘	shadow in orange
橘在橘旁	orange next to orange
橘在屋宇	orange on the roof
日落西方	sun sets in west
橘在野	orange in wilderness
日落橘	sunset in orange
苍茫在橘	gray falls in orange
月在屋檐	moon in the eaves
夜无橘	night without orange

(the transliteration imitates the original shape but there are extra syllables in thr English words while Chinese is monosyllabic)

It appears to be in the simple short-lined form of Shi Jing style (*Book of Songs*, 11th to 7th century BCE) but strangely enough it also echoes the seven syllable quatrains in the Tang Dynasty, only that it's fragmented as "XXXX / XXX" (日出东南 / 橘在野). (I use orange instead of tangerine because the o in orange resembles a sun.) The "wilderness" functions as a direction for the orange whether the sun rises in the Southeast or sets in the West. The orange faces the wilderness. A sun in itself. Orange on the roof, therefore daytime. Night with Orange, therefore nighttime. Orange and its shadow form a new yin yang, yellow orange and gray orange, first day of orange-kind like the first day of humankind.

Ezra Pound said, "Poetry is news that stays news." What's most interesting is the verb "stay". Poems from the *Book of Songs* and their styles speak to us today after three thousand years because of the universal value presented in the form of simplicity and condensed language. However, returning to the ancient minimalism is not all that Chinese poets are making efforts at. Apart from the form, contents and imageries are also what many poets are trying to make new. Chen Jun 陈均 (b1974) may have sounded like the post-Qing dynasty style but when I look closely at his poems, I find them going much further into the antique mode of imagination and sensibilities:

悲伤集

悲伤是坐在马背上，
缓缓前行，雨云低低地
碰触我们的头顶。

我们在白夜里睡不着觉，
一路上谈恋爱的颜色，
开玩笑的燕子忽前忽后。

应该诚实、更加诚实的劳作，
你的单纯中蕴含着微妙，
是啊，海大，海太寂寞。

地球记得你，记得每一颗粒子，
你已消瘦的手指向朝露，
笑着祝愿书比自己多活一年。

如今我独自又在绕海一周，
白沫可是飞鸟永不逝去的感念？
话语还夹杂在浪涛的喧嚣里。

    2010/5/5

BOOK OF THE SADNESS

Sadness moves slowly as if on a horseback
forward, forward, the rainy clouds are low
touching our foreheads.

We can't fall asleep at the white night,
so we talk about colors of love—
mischievous swallows flying around us.

Be honest. And be even more honest at work.
Your simple life embraces subtleties.
Yes, the ocean is big, and lonely.

The earth will remember you and every particle of you.
Your thinning hand waves to the morning dew,
wishing the book will live one year longer than yourself.

Now I've circled the ocean one more time.
Are the white foams the ever-green gratitude of a flying bird?
The discourse is mingled with loud waves.

This is a poem of mourning but with enchanting images. The poetic music is made possible with modern long lines. It's definitely not a rewrite of ancient poetry. It's a blending of the classical "horseback", "rainy clouds", "thinning hand", and "morning dew" with contemporary discourses such as "we talk about colors of love", "Now I've circled the ocean one more time", etc. etc. The ending is absolutely beautiful, a hybrid of ancient and current.

Chinese New Poetry started as a literary revolution a hundred years ago influenced by the new poetry that appeared in the *Poetry* magazine in Chicago. Hu Shi was a student in the US from 1910 to 1917. He wrote the first Chinese free verse in vernacular speech in July 1916, published "A Tentative Proposal of Literary Reform" in the *New Youth* journal in China in January 1917, followed by eight free verses in the same journal the next month, and returned to China in July to promote the New Poetry. This literary revolution was preceded by the downfall of the Qing dynasty in 1911 and reinforced by the May Fourth Cultural Movement in 1919. Poets in China today are celebrating 2017 as the one hundred year anniversary of New Poetry. But how do we re-evaluate Hu Shi and the other earlier modernists in China? How do we re-evaluate our New Poetry tradition? And how do we revitalize the ancient tradition? These are some of the issues we are facing today. Most serious poets are constantly striving to come up with something new. Looking back to the ancient is the current trend. A recent poem by Xi Du 西渡 (b1967) is a nice example of the new efforts. The poem sounds very classical but in contemporary free verse:

瓯鹭

海偶尔走向陆地，折叠成一只海鸥。
陆地偶尔走向海，藏身于一艘船。
海和陆地面对面深入，经过雨和闪电。
在云里，海鸥度量；
在浪里，船测度。
安静的时候，海就停在你的指尖上
望向你。
海飞走，好像一杯泼翻的水
把自己收回，当你偶尔动了心机。

海鸥收起翅膀，船收起帆。
潮起潮落，公子的白发长了，
美人的镜子瘦了。

一队队白袍的僧侣朝向日出。
一群群黑色的鲸鱼涌向日落。

　　　　　2016/04/07

SEABIRD

Sometimes the sea roams to the land, folded as a seagull.
Sometimes the land walks to the sea, hiding in a boat.
The sea and land go deeper to each other through rain and lightning.
In the clouds seagulls measure things.
In the waves boats too.
When it's quiet and calm, the sea stops on your fingertips
looking at you,

and then flies away like a cup of water poured
but retrieving itself when you start to care, even just slightly,
about worldly matters.

Seagulls gather their wings, boats their sails.
With the rise and fall of tides, the nobleman's gray hair gets long
and the beauty's mirror gets thin

while crowds of white robed monks rush to the sunrise
and flocks of black whales to the sunset.

Here the "nobleman" and "beauty" may sound cliché to Westerners, but the archaic words serve as a timeframe of when and where this poem is situated. The story comes from the Yellow Emperor Chapter of the Han Dynasty book *Liezi* and there have been many ancient poems about it throughout the centuries. The contemporary moral lesson is that only when you are unconcerned about worldly matters, such as fame or awards, will seabirds fly to you and even stay in your hands. When you have motivations and intentions in the earthly world, life will be difficult, you might as well do nothing as the Daoist saying goes, "the utmost doing is doing nothing" and the modern irony is that everyone is trying so hard to do things and their hair grows gray.

Look how the rhythms are built into the poem. It starts with a slow pace with the repetition of "sometimes" and moves faster with the symmetrical corresponding pairs as in typical classical couplets: sea and land, seagull and boat, wings and sails, white and black, etc. It moves faster and faster as the stanzas get shorter: they hurry and try to get the most out of life, as suggested by the "rush" towards the end. Even the white-robed monks (the imagery of waves) rush to the sunrise. They have forgotten that the more you want the less you get. But there is no preaching in the poem. The job is done through the allusion of the classical "seabird" story and a series of rhetorical strategies. The mirror is getting "thin" instead of the beauty's face. The object becomes the subject. You watch the mirror and the mirror becomes you. As you notice you are getting thinner, the mirror shrinks. As you observe, the seagulls and boats become subjects too. It's still the same seaside, but the perspective is changing and moving, which is typical in Chinese classical poetry.

The most interesting part is in the first line. In Chinese, "sea some(times)" (海偶(尔)) and "seagull" (海鸥) sound similar in such an utterly unusual way, something totally different echoes to each other, *hai ou, hai ou,* which makes them almost interchangeable. As the sea roams, it folds itself as a seagull, i.e. sometimes sea, sometimes a seagull. Therefore in line 6 "the sea stops on your fingertips" and in line 8 "(the sea) flies away". Notice the amazing zoom-in: "like a cup of water."

Modern Chinese has changed over time. Words evolved from monosyllabic to multisyllabic, unable to fit into the fixed metrical scheme or else the poem will sound like a doggerel. But the ancient outlook of life, the poetics and rhetoric can all be used today and used better. It's up to you how to make it new and it's testing your creativity and imagination. Dai Weina is a young female poet with intelligence and beauty and courage and, above all, a unique poetic voice with a fresh combination of words and beyond-this-planet imagination.

帐子外面黑下来（截选）

太多星星被捉进帐子里
它们的光会咬疼凡间男女
便凿一方池塘，散卧观它们粼粼的后裔
你呢喃的长发走私你新发明的性别
把我的肤浅一一贡献给你
白帐子上伏着一只夜
你我抵足，看它弓起的黑背脊

2015.6.18

OUTSIDE THE MOSQUITO NET THE DARKNESS FALLS

Too many stars are captured in the mosquito net
Their light bites the mortal men and women
So they dig a pond and lie around watching their sparkling descendants
You smuggle your newly invented gender
in your whispering long hair
And I give you my skin-deep shallowness, an offering to you
On top of the white net crouches a tiger of night
You and I, foot in foot, watch its curved back, black

Crouch is an interesting verb for night. The night crouches on top of the white mosquito net. She gives the quantifying word for mosquitos and tigers to the night (一只夜) as if night is a huge mosquito, as big as a tiger, crouching above her. As a matter of fact, every single line in this short stanza has something beautiful. Imagine the stars from a mosquito net at night and you will feel so close to them or them close to you as if they are inside your net. Look at how the verb "bite" bites. And the sparkling fish descendants as if mermaids can be born out of stars. The "newly invented gender" is what I like most. The day of you are either-a-woman-or-not is over. A third gender is born. As a contemporary young poet, she uses many archaic words and make them outstanding in lines. For instance, 抵足 foot in foot (I made this translation based on "arm in arm", "hand in hand") is a classical way of saying "two people sleep in the same bed with feet touched." Very intimate. But she cuts off the "sleep" segment of the ancient phrase and makes it sound new.

Why is that most of the ambitious poets in China aspire to revitalize ancient Chinese in a modern and post-modern way? What really is Chineseness? What is Native poetry? Did Hu Shi call to get rid of the old cultures including everything from the far ancient time? It is highly possible that we have misread Hu Shi for one hundred years. Reading his diaries I notice that he compared his literary reform to the Renaissance in the West. He was calling for a revitalization of the vernacular language from the ancient China. What he discarded were the ridged metrical frames of Chinese poetry, i.e. the cages for the free flow of ideas and words. As I see it, what some poets are doing today is not against the new tradition he set, but continuing that Renaissance and even starting a new one. And this effort started in the 1980s by several poets such as Zang Di:

房屋与梅树

毕竟存在过那样的时刻
房间里的女人还很年轻
她站立不动在四月的窗前
瘦削的双肩栖落两只白鸽

其实很可能并没有白鸽
而是她那花枝般的姿态
让我们感到露水滋润的安宁
血液凝结就像暗红的辣肠

那些梅花繁星般饱满
把春天最初的盛开移近她的面庞
甚至通过她鲜明的凝神注目
构成那房间里最深湛的秘密

    1984

ROOM AND A PLUM TREE

There was a moment after all
when the woman in the room was young
standing still before the window of April
On her slim shoulders landed two white pigeons

But perhaps there were no pigeons

It was her branching body
that made us feel the dew-wet tranquility
And her blood condensed like our crimson interior

The plum tree bloomed like full stars
illuminating her face with its first flowering
and through her glowing gaze
framed the bluest mystery in that room

Of all the classical imageries, "plum tree" takes the most prominent position and plum flower is regarded as Chinese flower. The mysterious woman in the poem can be the one giving birth to the author or someone he was in love with. Her "branching body" and "slim shoulders" are typical description of females in classical imaginations, the white doves are also ancient literary images. How a poem with all these ancient elements sounds so Western and contemporary is a mystery. Zhang Zao 张枣 (1962-2010) wrote more poems of this style, refined and Western-flavored language with Chinese classical images. While the above poem by Zang Di is almost obsolete, "Mirror" by Zhang Zao is enormously popular for whatever reasons:

镜中

只要想起一生中后悔的事
梅花便落了下来
比如看她游泳到河的另一岸
比如登上一株松木梯子
危险的事固然美丽
不如看她骑马归来
面颊温暖
羞惭。低下头，回答着皇帝
一面镜子永远等候她
让她坐到镜中常坐的地方
望着窗外，只要想起一生中后悔的事

梅花便落满了南山
　　1984

MIRROR

Plum flowers fall whenever a regret awakes—
as in watching her swim to the other shore
or climb a pinewood ladder.
Dangerous things are beautiful;
it's better to see that she returns on a horseback,
her face warm,
abashed, her head lowered, speaking back to the Emperor.
A mirror awaits her, as always,
allowing her to sit inside it, in her usual place,
and gaze out the window—regrets awaken all the plum flowers
as they fall, like egrets, over the South Hills.

  The traditional functions of Chinese language—pictographic, ideographic, sound-imitating, meaning-transferring, and so on—have always been played with in Chinese poetry as rhetorical devices. Instead of writing a long footnote about how the two key words, Plum (梅) and Regret (悔), resemble each other in shape and echo each other in sound, I added "like egrets" to demonstrate the aesthetics of this poem and how one thing resonates with another as in "regret" and "egret". What general readers find interesting is the "Emperor", something that has disappeared since the end of the last dynasty in China in 1911. One can see immediately the difference between using "Emperor" as a character in the poem and using a literary allusion such as in Xi Du's poem "Seabird" or creative use of "foot in foot" as in Dai Weinas poem. But of course there are other poems by Zhang Zao that are much more sophisticated and innovative than the one cited here. He was no doubt one of the pioneer poets who tried to bring the Chinese tradition back to life, making the old sound contemporary.

Most of the poems in 倪志娟 Ni Zhijuan's new book, "Hunting" 《猎·物》, are short pieces resembling the classical poems in tone and spirit. The book opens with "Swing":

秋千

先是颜色褪去
唇上的花
抽象成线条简单的微笑
她伸出手，握住岁月的流沙
流沙亦散去
她握住自己的手
在思想的绳索上荡秋千

2005/12/20

SWING

First the color fades away
Then the flower on her lips extracted
into a simple smile of abstract lines
She reaches out to hold the quicksand of hours
but it's dispersed quickly
She holds on to her own hand and takes a swing ride
on the ropes of her own thinking

Swing is an ancient form of recreational sports, "imported" to China in the 7th century BCE but it's also very common nowadays, a symbol of free movement. Life is fragile, time flows away. The only thing you can hold on is your own hand and your own thoughts. It echoes ancient wisdom but it runs through contemporary imagery and contemporary vocabulary. It's short and light, with a weight at the end. It brings me to the decade effort by Jiang Hao 蒋浩 (b1971), a poet born in Sichuan, after wandering for many years finally settled down in the South Sea

Island of China. While wandering around he wrote poems and tried many different ways to sound "ancient".

In the following poem by Jiang Hao, he wrote fourteen lines in the Upper part and fourteen lines again in the Lower part. A division of Upper and Lower used to be popular in the Song dynasty. Observation first, then philosophical thinking and free association. In the long sequence of "Poem of Wandering Immortals" written over the years of wandering, Jiang Hao has made most of the upper parts metaphysical, and most of the lower parts physical (upper as in the brain and lower as in the lower body) with some random exceptions. The fourteen lines are not sonnets but in his home-made structure of 5 – 5 – 4. In other words, he is making his "turning" point of the Song dynasty standard "opening, responding, turning, and closing" at a different point than the regular compositions, thus achieving a "freshness". The abundant use of archaic vocabulary mixed with contemporary jargons and strange imagination makes the poems almost "new classical". Is this the New Chinese poetry of the 21st century I have imagined? I ask myself. Is this poetry? I echo his own question.

游仙诗

上

不小心，和衣而眠时，裹挟了粉刺
和花序。狮子座垂下嫩枝，注射
万有引力到一苇之身。飘起来的
仙人球，在肥皂泡里，出神地褪刺；
浴巾的四只无忧角，挑逗四季轮回。

暮春或晚秋，意外地，编一只竹雀，
啄食水电站涟漪里隐忍的核动力：
一圈一年，在循环论里栽种藕荷。
谷底的大舌头像晾在枝杈的白裤衩，

生铁黑闸吞吐着煅烧过的瞥瞥劫波。

或掬水浇头，讨头彩；或量体裁衣，
合六合。幽闭在棒喝里的避雷针，
缝纫长亭短亭，直到爬山虎骑墙，
拱伏政治；火烧云拦路，除名道统。

下

呵，道通呢？厨房乳房。云，漆黑
城垛般的围裙；星坠油锅，炼铁。
油盐酱醋，阴阳交错，盘里竖起
一座桥。美不美，看桥墩？割草机
舔着下水道，篱笆扎在蜂腰不知处。

你好食如色如德，采薇歌露台不老，
用虹吸管隔山啜饮愈合的枯山水，
请红线女点起佛跳墙时的鬼吹灯。
姜葱蒜貌似你我他，烹出一地鸡毛；
碗里盘里，都是解体后复制的配偶。

呵，菜谱妖里妖气，藏了饕餮程序；
绘本难堪古雅，起皱的皮肤挽留
骤起的云雨，望远镜颠倒了蜃楼。
临帖之手，往咖啡里掺墨。这是诗？

    2010/5/25，金盘

POEM OF WANDERING IMMORTALS

Upper

He lies down with clothes on, accidentally catching thorns
and blossoms, young branches hanging down from Leo
as if injecting gravity into the body of a reed. A floating
cactus, in soap bubbles, gets rid of its needles unconsciously

while the bath towel finds no worries on its four horns,
provoking four seasons of reincarnations.

It's late spring or autumn. A bamboo bird, incidentally,
pecks at the nuclear power from the enduring ripples
of the hydropower plant: one circle a year, planting lotus
like practicing a cyclical theory. The valley's mouth resembles
a white undergarment on a branch, the black iron gate outputs
burning waves of catastrophes.

You either shower your top like winning a top lottery
or tailor to your body's six corners and win a Mark Six.
A lightning rod hides in a drinking bar. A sewing machine
sews pavilions, long and short, until a climbing ivy
ambushes politics; a fire cloud blocks the way removing
all moralities and authorities.

Lower

Oh a passage? A kitchen with floating breasts. Clouds.
Dark aprons like battling cities. Stars fall into an oil pan
forging iron. Soy sauce and vinegar stagger like
yin and *yang*. On the plate a bridge stands up.
Beautiful? Like a pier? A lawn mower licks the sewer,
a fence built in nowhere of its bee slim waist.

You love food, love its lusty colors, its ingredients as integrities.
On the cherry cheerful terrace a straw draws water
from a dried out tree, inviting the red thread girl to light up
the ghost lamp when a Buddhist jumps over the wall.
Gingers, leeks and garlics look like him and you and me, a floor of
chicken feathers. Bowls and dishes and plates, spouses of
replications.

Ah the recipes possess a gluttonous order like demons.
The picture books look embarrassingly ancient
and stylish. All those wrinkled skins have retained
stormy rains. In the telescope is an upside down mirage
where a drawing hand is stirring ink in the coffee.
Is this poetry?

* The poems are translated by the author of this essay, Ming Di.

风乎舞雩，东西东兮（代后记）

　　西方对中国古诗的翻译，引起中国热，而催生了象征主义，颓废派，超现实主义，意象派等多种现代风格；现代派的自由体又催生了中国白话新诗。胡适的第一首白话诗《答梅觐庄——白话诗》不仅具有20世纪初的现代性，同时也很奇妙地具有当下的后现代性，比如最近10年欧美很流行的多文体穿插和裁剪拼贴，胡适早就实验了。庞德于1913年发表于美国《诗刊》的两行诗《地铁站》，1917年诗刊主编门罗女士并没有收入她编选的《新诗》选集里，但后来被公认为现代派代表作品，中国新诗对胡适的认识却晚了一百年。白话新诗对抗明清八股文，追随现代派自由体和呼吸节奏，英美现代派对抗十四世纪以来的抑扬格五音步，以及乔治王时代和维多利亚时代的僵化文风，美学上对抗浪漫主义之后在当时流行的现实主义，也就是说，实验派诗人既要对抗传统积淀，又要对抗当下流行，还要对付革新障碍。

　　中国早期现代派的作品直到九十年代才被重新发现、重视。七十年代的中国汉语诗呈现的是前现代美学趣味，而这种美学趣味多年来在国际上代表着中国当代诗。九十年代的重大变化尚未较全面地译介出去，新世纪又出现新的流变和美学追求，即如何打通古今，这在八十年代就是暗流，分支，到了新世纪凸显出来。

　　《诗东西》从2010年开始探索一种中西对话式的文本编选，有中外诗人互译等栏目。创办《风》并不是要改吹中国风，或者复古风，不具有现代性的一味复古绝不是风刊的方向。办此刊的想法也萌生于2010年，但由于当时迷恋于互译形式而主打《诗东西》，现在终于启动《风》。

　　风——某种美学倾向的同人诗刊，2016年12月25日正式创刊，标志为：

风刊想让 Feng 这个汉语拼音像 Fengshui 一样成为世界语，颠覆一切对当代中国诗的陈旧认识。从诗东西，到风这个东西，性质没变，尽管有脱胎换骨的感觉。

《风》诗刊诞生，正值新诗百年。思考"断裂"问题，首先与当下断裂，寻找新的缝隙。风，风雅，风雅颂，风骚，风流，风气，风潮，风味，风格，风姿，风度，风言风语，风情，风光，风韵，风骨，风声，风化，风车，风凉，风向，风波，风采，风范，风貌，风险，风景，风湿，风邪，风马牛，风什么都是，也可以什么都不是，只是风。中国古代第一姓，伏羲女娲都姓风。风，企图飞到远古，但并非通常意义上的古风，风首先是流动的，运动的物象，古中今外自由穿行。风形成气候，改变事物；从国风开始，风，流变成一种美学概念，风诗刊注入新生。

确切说，风不是飞回古代，而是载古飞行，飞向新的维度。

风拒绝妥协，敢于冒犯。

风即使朝着同一个方向吹，风之间也具有个体风格差异，而且同一个作者也会呈现不同的风貌：轻风，微风，和风，清风，强风，疾风，烈风，狂风，飓风，台风，龙卷风。即使是同一阵风，也有不同的速度，力度。

风拒绝平面，追求差异。

风拒绝平庸，追求奇异。

风拒绝平淡，追求陌异。

风拒绝平浅，追求诡异。

风，自然是飘逸的。但可以造出易经的易。

风拒绝平常，追求极端。

风拒绝高大上，一意孤行颓废。

风决绝于现实，穿透世事。

超现实主义，玄幻，唯美，是我们某些人的嗜好，但又穿越这些。

反讽，是我们某些人的匕首，但刀刃隐藏。

身体，身体，形而上貌似缴械，身体写作从我们真正开始。

立体主义，是我们的前辈，我们只会做的更好。

语言，是我们的工具，也是我们的思维，更是我们的眼睛。

视觉的，听觉的，嗅觉的，味觉的，触觉的——
风，具有可以感知的巨大的能量。

风，又是微小的，安静的，无形无体，几乎看不见。但期待摧枯拉朽。

《风》不顺着任何风，而是逆风而行的风。每个诗人都是带电粒子，因某种磁场作用而流动，飞翔，聚集成风。我们期待第二卷、第三卷新人加盟。

甲骨文的"风"是一只高飞的鹏鸟，后演化成虫，风生虫还是虫生风？虫即龙，龙卷风即飞旋的中国鸟。正如风的本义是使鸟飞翔起来的气流，一种自然气象，风诗刊也旨在与飞鸟/飞龙一起形成一种具有中国诗风的物象。

2016 年 12 月 25 日

Preview of next issue 下期预告

THEIR POEMS AND THEIR PAINTINGS

Jike Bu (1986-, birth name Jike Ayibujin), Yi nationality, born and grew up in Xichang, Sichuan province, went to college in Chengdu and graduate school in Chongqing, first Yi woman specializing in art. Currently she teaches art in Xichang Normal College, the only college in the Big Cold Mountain region. She started publishing poems while in college and became known as one of the best Yi poets of the younger generation. Jike Bu speaks Yi as her mother tongue but writes poetry in Han Chinese.

Call Her Suoma*

Call her Suoma
in the name of love we share
in the last, this and next life.
Love her—love her breathtaking color
         from blooming,
the traces she left
in the wind the rain the scorching sun.
Nothing distains her beauty: she is pure
like ice jade
but she is not just pretty and frail.
Her sonorous voice comes from the air,
the revolving stream, the soil.
Love her.
And embrace her barren body
like heaven and earth
and everything that grows on earth
with natural birth and death
in the world even though the world
doesn't care where the wind blows,
where you're from what you are or where you're going.
She has her own garden, her old dream
and her clearly sounded name—
Call her Suoma out loud
like calling yourself.

Translated from the Chinese by Ming Di

*Suoma means Azalea flower in Yi language. It's also the most common name for women in the Yi region in China.